AF350771

Jean-Marc ARACTINGI

The Hidden Face of the Druze

"The Freemasons of the East"

Biographie de l'Auteur

Jean-Marc Aractingi is a former Minister Plenipotentiary of the Central African Republic for Lebanon and the Arab Countries.

Currently, he is Director of the Chair of Religious Esotericism and Christology at the Instituto Sancti Pauli - Saint Peter & Saint Paul Lutheran Institute (Canada).

Doctor in Theology and History of Religions from International Christian University, he is an Engineer-Diplomat by training.

Engineer from AgroParisTech, he specializes in solar energy and completes his engineering training by preparing a Doctorate in thermal engineering at the Ecole Centrale de Paris; DEA in Development from the University of Paris I - Sorbonne, he also graduated from the 3rd cycle in Superior Diplomacy from the Center for Diplomatic and Strategic Studies of Paris (Doctoral School) and a former intern at the École de Guerre (formerly the Interarmed College Defense).

Former Lecturer at ISAA (School of Application of AgroParisTech and École Polytechnique) and at the University of Paris VIII and former CEO of the ARCORE-SOLARCORE SA Group, leader in solar engineering in the Middle-East , he is the President of the Franco-Arab Association of Graduates of Grandes Écoles (ENA, X, HEC, AgroParisTech, Mines, Centrale ...).

Freemason (33rd REAA, CBCS, 96th, 7th RO), he was initiated in 1986 in Lebanon then exalted Master at the Grand Lodge of France in the Orient of Paris and corresponding member of the famous Jean Scot Erigène Research Lodge of the Grand Lodge of France.

He is currently Sovereign Grand Commander of the Supreme Arab Masonic Council, World Grand Master of the Grand Orient Arab and Grand Master of the Sovereign Grand Order of Egyptian Rites for Lebanon.

Medalist of the Order of Merit of the Great World Hierophany, he is High Dignitary of the Sovereign International Shrine of the Egyptian Rites of Memphis-Misraïm, President of the Great World Hierophany for Arab Countries and member of the Leadership of the World Masonic Union of the 33rd degree of the REAA.

Grand Cross of the Order of Saint Paul; Grand Cross and Grand Commander of the Order of Lafayette, he is also a Knight of the Order of Malta-Grand Priory of Russia and of the Order of the Temple.

From the same author

– L'Indispensable du chineur des Peintres Orientalistes (Éd. Vues d'Orient, Paris, 2003).

– La Politique à mes trousses (Éd. L'Harmattan, Paris, 2006).

– Secrets initiatiques en Islam et rituels maçonniques (Éd. L'Harmattan, Paris, 2008).

– Rituels et catéchismes au Rite Œcuménique (Éd. L'Harmattan, Paris, 2011).

– Islam et Franc-Maçonnerie-Traditions ésotériques (Éd. Edilivre-Paris, 2014).

– Histoire mondiale de la franc-maçonnerie en terre d'islam, tome I, Turquie-Egypte-Iran (Éd. Érick Bonnier-Collection Encre d'Orient, Paris, 2016).

– Histoire mondiale de la franc-maçonnerie en terre d'islam, tome II, Liban-Syrie-Palestine (Éd. Erick Bonnier – Collection Encre d'Orient, Paris, 2016)

– Le Rite Œcuménique (Judéo-Chrétien-Musulman) en Franc-Maçonnerie

Tome I (2017 - Amazon Kindle Direct Publishing)

– L'Islam ésotérique et spirituel en 7 leçons (2017 - Amazon Kindle Direct Publishing)

– Dictionnaire des Francs-Maçons Arabes et Musulmans (2018 - Amazon Kindle Direct Publishing)

– Dictionary of Arab & Muslim Freemasons (2018 – Amazon CreateSpace Independent Publishing Platform)

– Jésus-Christ dans l'Islam à la lumière des découvertes de la Mer Morte et des Évangiles Apocryphes (2019- Amazon CreateSpace Independent Publishing Platform)

– Histoire de la Franc-Maçonnerie au Moyen-Orient (Liban – Syrie – Palestine – Turquie – Egypte – Iran…) (2019 – Amazon CreateSpace Independent Publishing Platform)

Some collaborations:

– Les Druzes et la Franc-maçonnerie, in Les Cahiers de l'Orient, N° 69, 1er trimestre 2003, Paris : L'Équerre et le Croissant, éditions Les Cahiers de l'Orient.

– Points de convergence dans les rituels et symboles chez les Druzes et chez les Francs-maçons, in Les Cahiers Jean Scot Erigène, N° 8, Franc-Maçonnerie et Islamité, Paris : La Grande Loge de France.

Table of contents

Chapitre I

An Enigmatic Origin

The Druze do not seem to constitute an ethnic group insofar as the first of them were probably Muslims (Ismailis from the Maghreb, Islamized Copts) then after the exodus joined the movement of Muslims from Syria, sometimes from the Arabian Peninsula, or the Kurds.

It is their belonging to a heterodox spiritualist current of Islam, then of its Shiite component, near its Ismaili branch, which marks those whom it is agreed to call the Druze and who are called, among themselves, "Unitarists" (Mouwahidoun).

Their respect for religion does not require following the "five pillars of Islam", praying in a Sunni or Shiite mosque; their legal system is distinct from "sharia", and their adherence to reincarnation, which they share with Alawis and Ismailis, alienates them from all other Muslims.

Their scholars meet in closed premises, where the public cannot go, apart from the initiates, which led Gérard de Nerval in his "Voyage en Orient" to call them "the Freemasons of the East".

Emergence of Druzism

Genealogy:

- Ali (652-661), husband of Fatima, daughter of Muhammad
- Husayn (669-680)
- Ali Zayn al Abidin (680-712)
- Muhammad Al Bakir (712-743)
- Ja'far al Sadiq (743-765)
- Ismaïl (died in 762 ?)
- Muhammad al-Maktum (died in 813)
- Ahmad al-Wafi(813-828)
- Muhammad al-Taqi (828-840)
- Abdallah al-Radi (840-881)

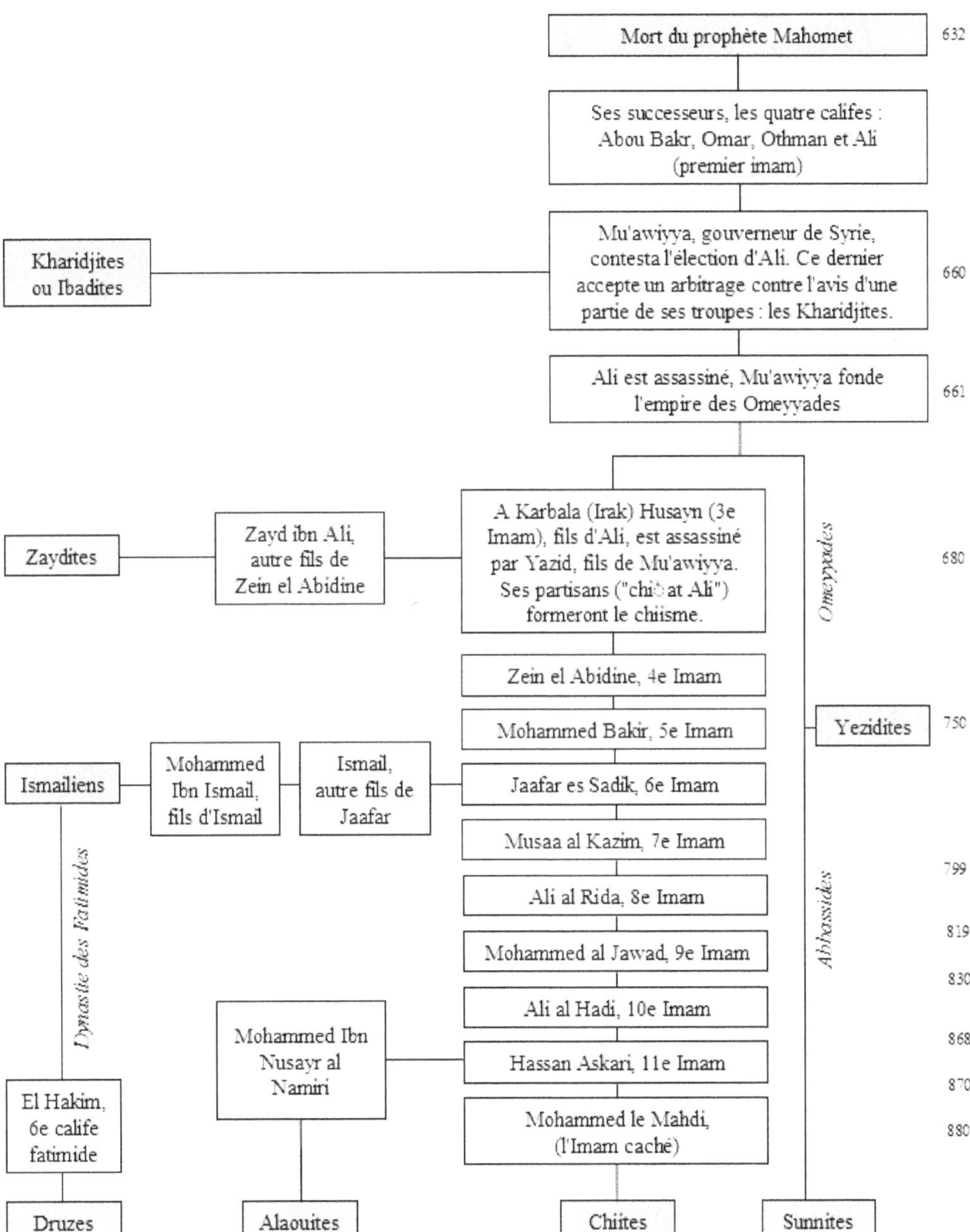

Mort du prophète Mahomet
632
Ses successeurs, les quatre califes :
Abou Bakr, Omar, Othman et Ali
(premier imam)
Kharidjites
ou Ibadites
Mu'awiyya, gouverneur de Syrie,
contesta l'élection d'Ali. Ce dernier
accepte un arbitrage contre l'avis d'une
partie de ses troupes : les Kharidjites.
660
Ali est assassiné, Mu'awiyya fonde
l'empire des Omeyyades
661
Zaydites
Zayd ibn Ali,
autre fils de
Zein el Abidine
A Karbala (Irak) Husayn (3e
Imam), fils d'Ali, est assassiné
par Yazid, fils de Mu'awiyya.
Ses partisans ("chi at Ali")
formeront le chiisme.
Omeyyades
680
Zein el Abidine, 4e Imam
Mohammed Bakir, 5e Imam
Yezidites
750
Ismailiens
Mohammed
Ibn Ismail,
fils d'Ismail
Ismail,
autre fils de
Jaafar
Jaafar es Sadik, 6e Imam
Musaa al Kazim, 7e Imam
Dynastie des Fatimides
Ali al Rida, 8e Imam
Abbassides
799
Mohammed al Jawad, 9e Imam
819
830
Mohammed Ibn
Nusayr al
Namiri
Ali al Hadi, 10e Imam
868
Hassan Askari, 11e Imam
870
El Hakim,
6e calife
fatimide
Mohammed le Mahdi,
(l'Imam caché)
880
Druzes
Alaouites
Chiites
Sunnites

Around the 900s, an Iranian living in Syria, Obaydallah impersonates the grandson of Ismail, son of Jaafar, the 6th Shiite imam.

The particular "Ismaili" Islam develops an esoteric, hermetic, Platonic doctrine but also of free-thought acquired by successive initiations.

Obaydallah is called to Tunis by propagandists, and he will create a dynasty in a new capital, Mahdiya.

His descendants decide to conquer Egypt closer to the rival Abbasid empire.

In 969, the Fatimid caliph Al Mu'izz was delivered Egypt and founded "Cairo", (Al Qahira), from the name of the planet Mars, called "The Victorious" in Arabic, which, at that time, was rising. in the firmament according to astrologers.

The Fatimid dynasty will now reign in Cairo.

1- Obaydallah al-Mahdi (881-934)
2- Al-Qâ'im (934-946)
3- Al Mansour (946-952)
4- Al Mu'izz (952-975)
5- Al Aziz (975-996)
6- Al Hakim (996-1021)

The sixth Caliph Al Hakim Bi-Amrallah, born August 13, 985, was enthroned on September 13, 996, at the age of 11.

At the time he was born, all the planets were united in the sign of Cancer, and Saturn presided over the hour in which he was born.

We will see the importance of this event in the Druze Cosmogony later.

It was on May 30, 1017 that he announced the start of a new era and affirmed his own divine character.

Undoubtedly, it is one of his preachers Hamza Ibn Ali of Iranian origin, claiming to be born the same day in Suze as his sovereign, who organizes the statutes of this new religion, with his disciple Ali Ibn Ahmad alias Muqtanna Bahaedinne, nicknamed "The Regulator of Time" ("Qaym el Zamman").

Hamza introduced among the "Mouwahidoun" the influence of the Zoroaster and Mani cults.

Deified in this way, al Hakim will be challenged for his enigmatic and extravagant behavior, which only fascinates a handful of supporters.

So for some, he appears idealistic, mystical, divine, and for others, a ruthless tyrant, trying, in the name of a so-called ideal society, to merge all religions into one, and thus oppose the primacy of Islam.

Indeed, according to the Ismaili doctrine which considers the Imam as the personification of the cosmic Intellect, the God of the Koran, the do'at Hamza and Darazi saw in al-Hakim the last and ultimate manifestation of the divinity in the form of human.

In this capacity, he would have revoked all previous religions, including Islam, both in their apparent and literal aspect (Zahir) and in their hidden meaning (Batin).

Persecutions will ensue, against the Sunnis, summoned to renounce their rituals and to hear indictments in mosques against the first caliphs, the most respected, and against Christians who must wear distinctive clothing and a bell around their necks. .

All the more surprising, since Al Hakim's mother was a Christian, and his maternal uncle was a Patriarch according to generally accepted historical sources.

Indeed, the father of Caliph al-Hakim bi-Amr Allah, Caliph Abu Mansour al Aziz had two wives.

One of them was al Hakim's mother.

She was a Melkite Christian whose two brothers had been appointed Patriarchs of the Melkite Church by Caliph al Aziz.

Despite this parentage, al-Hakim bi-Amr Allah's relationship with Christians was tumultuous throughout the years of his rule.

Thus, at the beginning of his reign in 1004, he decreed a law ordering Jews and Christians to wear a rope tied around the waist and to have a badge of colored fabric, a sort of badge, and this , in order to be publicly distinguished from Muslims.

In the same year, al-Hakim took action against the slave traders, including preventing them from selling slaves and maids to Christians and Jews.

There were probably other steps taken at the time, or perhaps just a few signs of the Caliph's intention to impose even more difficult conditions.

His unexplained actions aroused great fear, especially among the officials, among whom were a large number of committed Christians and Jews.
As a group, the latter demonstrated their loyalty and begged al Hakim to forgive them.

However, it is quite difficult to know what they think should be forgiven.

However, they were received at the Palace and were pardoned and amnestied by a decree.

It is difficult to make sense of this event.

What caused the fear and panic that manifested themselves that year among Christians?

Was it the execution in 1002 of Fahd Ibrahim, one of their leader and who was the most prominent Christian in the government?

Fahd was accused of corruption, and his brother had tried to save him by paying a huge sum to the Caliph who refused him by ordering a few days after Fahd's death, the arrest and imprisonment of Christian clerics in the government. , before releasing them a week later at the personal request of

Sahl Muqashshar, his private doctor, himself a Christian.

Another factor that may have influenced Al Hakim's attitude towards Christians is that they were treated well in his father's time.

Al Aziz's favorite wife was, as seen above, a Melkite Christian, and her brother held, in part through her intervention, important positions in the Christian community.

Al Aziz's favorite daughter, Sitt al Mulk (who will take power in the year 1021 when al-Hakim "disappears", continued to maintain her father's policy of tolerance towards Christians. , which was not the case with his half-brother al Hakim.

His mother's brother, Arsenius, who was previously the Metropolitan in Cairo, was promoted to the rank of Patriarch of Alexandria upon the death in the year 1000 of the previous holder of that post, but this was not necessarily a sign of Al Hakim's personal approval.

On the contrary, Caliph al-Hakim continued to persecute Christians and in the year 1008, on the night of Palm Sunday, he forbade Christians to decorate their Churches as they used to do.

Many Crosses have been stolen from the churches and have been burned at the doors of mosques and in police stations.

This measure seemed to target as much the practice of the Christian faith as the churches and their property.

Worse, it was that same year in 1008 that Caliph Al-Hakim bi-Amr Allah ordered the destruction of the Church of the Holy Sepulcher in Jerusalem.

These discriminatory measures against Christians will increase during these years:
In 1010, for example, Christians were prohibited from celebrating Epiphany.

In fact, they were not to congregate on the banks of the Nile as they used to. In 1011, they were forbidden to assemble for the feast of the Cross and several Churches were destroyed (during the years 1012 to 1015 more than thirty Churches and Monasteries were destroyed!).

Suddenly in 1013, and for no apparent reason, Caliph al-Hakim announced that all protected persons, such as Christians, were now free to leave his kingdom and take with them all their possessions and whatever they could carry.

For the Melkites, this offer allowed them to leave Fatimid territory and settle in the Byzantine Empire, notably in the city of Antioch located in northern Syria.

For the Copts they may have gone south, to Nubia or Ethiopia, two predominantly Coptic Christian countries.

Historian Yahya, who later became Melkite Bishop of Antioch, is one of those who left during this time.
Certainly many others have left Egypt for more hospitable countries.

Later, towards the end of his reign, al Hakim also began to moderate his policy towards Christians, allowing those who had converted to Islam to revert to their original religion, if they so desired.

Christian homes that were destroyed were rebuilt with his permission.

There is not enough information about this sudden change towards the Christians of Caliph Al Hakim which occurred during the last years of his reign is largely lacking.

One finds in "The History of the Coptic Patriarchs" a curious account of the affection of the Caliph for a monk who, once authorized to return to his Christian religion, asked for authorization to rebuild Churches and Monasteries.

Al Hakim granted them to him and frequently went to the Monastery to meet the Monk.
It will be the same for the Melkite Churches and Monasteries.

Note :

In one of the first Druze manuscripts to reach Europe entitled "Milad Mawlana al Hakim (Birth of Our Lord al-Hakim), it is mentioned that her mother was a descendant of Fatima, the daughter of the Prophet and not as we have just seen of a Christian mother, which would partly explain her behavior towards Christians.

In this manuscript we can read:

"Our Lord al-Hakim was the son of Ismail, descended from Ali bin Abi Talib.

Her mother was descended from the radiant Fatima, daughter of Muhammad bin Abdallah.

He was born in Misr (Egypt), on the night of Thursday 23 Rabi 'I in the year 375 AH (14 August 985).

His father designated him as his successor in the month of Chaabane in the year 383 (October 993).

He acceded to the caliphate on Thursday, the last day of Ramadan in the year 386 (December 996).

The duration of his reign was twenty-five years.

He entered into occultation on the night of Monday 27 Chawwal in the year 411 (13 February 1021).

The duration of his presence in this world, from his birth until his occultation, was thirty-six years and seven months.

He issued a venerable Edict and hung it in mosques, then he entered into occultation.

We expect his return shortly, if he wants to.

He will then reign over all the earth forever.

Those he called to profess his Oneness but who refused to do so - these are the followers of all sects and all religions - will be subject to him: each year, they will have to pay the poll tax and they will have to bear distinctive marks. On the other hand, those who professed his Oneness will reign with him forever.

We will now begin, with the permission of Our Lord al-Hakim, the exposition of our Druze doctrine, we who entered (indarazna) in the faith, after the religion of Muhammad bin Abdallah, the ruler of the Islamic Hegira.

May the curse of the Lord be upon him! ".

On the other hand, on the other hand, al-Hakim surrounded himself with intellectuals, founding the research institution Dar el Hikma, where the new "Druze" doctrine was developed (named after, it is said, a another of his al-Darazi disciples), whose spirituality is experienced without ritual constraint.

The Caliph passes for a divine emanation, a hypostasis.
But in his entourage, infighting will end the reign.

This Nachtakine Al Darazi, of Turkish origin, tries to replace the adviser Hamza Ibn Ali, during the year 1016.

The Caliph then suspended the campaign of proselytism and, on May 19, 1018, ceasing all profane and official activity, he retired to Mount Muqattam, in the desert east of Cairo in a mosque, called "Raydan".

Opponents come to assault, accusing the sovereign's advisers of all these dangerous innovations for the state.

The public reappearance of the Caliph calms the spirits.

Darazi disappears, either executed or having fled to the Lebanese-Syrian borders of Wadi el Taym, where he is said to have continued to convert new disciples.

In 1021, the Caliph disappeared once again.

His lacerated, bloody clothes will be found on the Muqattam.

Since the myth of occultation is redundant in Shiism, the disciples spread the news that Al Hakim is not deceased, but that, hidden from the eyes of men, he continues to rule them through the literati of the community.

Al Hakim's son, Caliph al Zaher, orders persecutions against his father's disciples for seven years.

In 1028, a letter from Hamza reopened a growing membership campaign outside of Egypt.

In 1036, Caliph Al Mustansir, put an end to the persecutions.

But in 1043, al Muqtanna compiled the "Books of Wisdom" of the "Unitarists" and closed all proselytism.

We are born Druze, we don't become Druze anymore.

Following this event, we can legitimately ask the following question:

The pastoral (Da'wa) Druze having ceased 60 years after the disappearance of Caliph Al Hakim, how were the families of new Druze formed after 1060 (435h)?
As we have just seen, Druzism having originated at the court of Caliph Al Hakim, of the Fatimid dynasty, founded in Tunisia by a Syrian Obaydallah.

Before leaving Mahdiya in Tunisia, the court was to be composed of Berbers, and by settling on the banks of the Nile, it received and assimilated a number of Egyptian notables.

After the disappearance of Caliph Al Hakim (1017), fleeing persecution, the Druze converts fled as we have seen in Palestine, Syria, Lebanon, in mountainous regions.

There they had to blend in with the local population, and no doubt the Druze community was transformed with the contribution of Sunni Arab tribes, the Tanoukh, Arslan, Bouhtourides, or Shiite clans of Hermel, such as the Hamadé.

Finally, the first Druze having disappeared, their descendants having mixed with denominational different inhabitants, even if they were Muslims, it was Druzism which attracted by its choice of society, its transmission of knowledge by initiation, and the distribution of its faithful into "scholars" and "ignorant", a distinction, it has been understood, not based scientifically but esoterically.

The Druzification of communities was often done for economic reasons, and by acquisition of land by inheritance.

A non-Druze son-in-law inherited from his stepfather Druze and became Druze.

This is why the Druze movement is part of the Arabian; its followers claim tribal origin, from Syria, even Iraq.

It was only after 400 years after the proclamation of the "Da'wa Druze" that the jurisprudence and legislation of the Druze community were codified, with the Sheikhs Jalaleddine, Fadhel, Amin el Sayyed, the Emir Saleh, all of the Tanoukh tribe.

Non-Druze feudal families continued, through the game of alliances, to acquire, by way of inheritance, their insertion into the Unitarian community.

Thus the son of Emir Ali Joumblatt, Sunni, married the daughter of Sheikh El Kadi, and inherited the land around Mukhtara in the 16th century.

Nevertheless, the Druze were not recognized by the Ottoman Empire of jurisprudence, nor of special personal status, and were considered fully Sunnis.

It is the Emir Majid Arslan, who, in 1948, obtained the creation of specific courts to settle the problems of marriage, divorce, inheritance, all the more so, as exceptionally in this part of the world, the woman enjoys a certain equality with the man for the distribution of the inheritance shares and the obtaining of the divorce.

Likewise, if political coordination functions were entrusted to the Sheikhs of Druze clans, they were not recognized as having any competence in the religious field, nor with regard to the transmission of a "baraka" or blessing, or of proselytizing actions.

Thus over the centuries, the Druze community no longer recognized itself in the founding fathers of Cairo, but benefited from the demographic contribution of populations migrating for economic or security reasons, and taking refuge in the regions. high less easily accessible to Ottoman occupants.

At the time of the mandate, Western educated Druze, intellectuals, began to participate in the management of the country, while the Druze fundamentalists maintained an attitude of disapproval for the rapid evolution of the elites in a profoundly changed secular world.

Flight from Egypt from the Druze

After the occultation of the one that the Druze consider as the 14th and last Imam (2 times 7), the new religious community will regroup in Wadi el Taym, near Mount Hermon, in Hauran (future Jebel Druze), and little little by little in the Lebanese Chouf.

The "Unitarists" will grow with the conversion of the Arab tribes originating from Yemen, settled in Syria in the 7th century, and therefore Sunnis, or Christianized, the Ghassanids.

On the other hand, coming from Iraq, the Maan clan, former leaders of the Qayssite party (the Arabs of the peninsula were traditionally divided into "Qayssites" and "Yemenites") settled in the Chouf, around 1120, in Deir el Qamar; some of its leaders would become local notables until the end of the 7th century (such as the Bouhtourides from 1147 to 1516).
Another component, this time Kurdish, the Tanoukh, followed later by the Arslan, Joumblatt or Takieddine.

At first, the Druze did not hesitate to conquer coastal territories; the Syrian town of Banias, for example, which they handed over to the Crusaders in 1129.

But in 1292 the Mamelukes of Egypt carried out a general offensive against all dissident Muslims.

They push back the Druze in Chouf, who will now be replaced in Kesrouan by the Maronites from the North, after their expulsion from Syria.

As for the Alaouites, they take refuge in Akkar.

In 1034, conquerors of the Mongols and the Crusaders, the Mamluks again engage in repressions against the Shiites, Druze and Alaouites.

At the battle of Sofar (1037), the Druze narrowly escaped extermination.

Forced to take refuge in increasingly inaccessible haunts, the two clans of Tanoukh and Maan will, through the play of regional political alliances (Damascus, Tripoli, Saida), develop an autonomy that will last until arrival of the Ottomans.

Fakhreddin (1572-1635) and relations with the West

It was in Mount Lebanon itself, around 1516, that a Maronite-Druze alliance developed, first directed against the Shiites, then against Turkish hegemony.

In 1523, the Ottoman governor of Damascus Khourram Pasha mounted an expedition which went to the Barouk region, burning 40 villages, massacring the inhabitants, and above all removing the secret books of the Druze to entrust them to Sunni theologians who learned about them for the first time.

Then the Ottoman forces withdrew and Emir Maan Fakhreddin I (1544) created a semi-independent family dynasty.

His son Qorqmaz died of grief in 1585 after witnessing a new invasion of Lebanon by the Turks.

His wife, Princess Nassab, entrusts her children, including the future Fakhreddin II, to the care and education of the Maronite princes El Khazen.

The one called the "great Fakhreddin" will not only defend Mount Lebanon against the Turks and other enemies, but also enlarge the national territory by occupying Safad and Ajloun in the Galilee thus controlling the road to Jerusalem.

He negotiated with the Medici of Tuscany an economic cooperation treaty, which the Turks disapproved of; temporarily leaving Lebanon to the regency of his eldest son, he went to Florence from 1613 to 1618, enjoying the welcome of the Tuscan family.

Back in Lebanon, he was baptized by a Carmelite Father.

His feats of arms will lead him to Palmyra.

But, in 1633, the Turks invaded Lebanon again, seizing Fakhreddin II and his sons Mansour, Haidar, Boulouk, whom they would execute in Istanbul in 1635.

This prince will remain in the eyes of the Lebanese as their first statesman, famous for his spirit of tolerance, the openness of his culture, and his militant nationalism.

In a colorful and touching way, Gérard de Nerval will say of him that he "represented the ideal that we form of Hiram", today one would have said of him "A Freemason without an apron".

The Maronites, like all of their compatriots, will benefit from these relations forged with the West; thus, by founding their College in Rome, will they prolong the action of their sovereign Druze?

After him, in deep difficulty, the Emirs Melhem, Qorqmaz and Ahmed followed one another.

In 1697, without male descendants, the latter will have as successors his cousins, the Emirs Chehab, themselves Sunnis from Wadi el Taym.

It was Bachir 1st Chehab (1697-1700) who was elected by the notables gathered at Samkaniyya (Shouf) and who was to found the new dynasty.

The Chehab Dynasty (1697-1840)

It was under Emir Chehab (1706-1729) that a political divide arose between Druze opposing the Ottomans, the Qayssites, and pro Turks, the Yemenis.

Their bloodiest clash took place in 1711, at Ain Dara, in which Maronite allies took part on both sides.

Under Emir Melhem (1725-1754), linked with Azm, Pasha de Damascus, fighting opposed Druze and Shiites, causing the latter to exodus from the Jezzine region.

Under Emir Youssef, Admiral Orlov's Russian fleet bombarded Beirut in 1711; the Chehabs had settled there since 1749.

From 1776 to 1804, Lebanon suffered the abuses of Al Jazzar, the ruthless Albanian governor of Acre, which Bonaparte could not overcome in 1799.

Interfaith relations between Druze and Maronites remain good; sometimes the families of Druze notables convert to Christianity, like the Abillamaa.

The image we have in the West at the time of the Druze is flattering because a fanciful etymology makes them descend from a crusader, the Duke of "Dreux"!

We see it in the correspondence of the Jesuit Fathers, published under the title Lettres Édifiantes:

"A French colony established for several centuries in Asia seemed to me to have piqued the curiosity of a French".

We are amazed at their spirit of tolerance, exceptional in the Ottoman Empire; This is how twelve Greek Catholic convents were built in Druze territory between 1720 and 1785, as Volney reports.

The dynasty ended with the long reign of Emir Bashir II (1788-1840).

The latter had to lead the small state under the threat of many constraints, inter-Druze rivalries, the hostility of Jazzar Pasha, Bonaparte's expedition, the Egyptian expansion leading to the occupation of Syria.

The already secular Druzo-Maronite understanding was to sink into new trials. In 1833, trouble broke out between Druze and Christians for the first time because of the occupation of their territory by the Egyptian troops of Mohamed Ali and the intrigues of the Sublime Porte.

In 1840, the Egyptian imposition of compulsory conscription raised the Druze and Maronites together.

Ibrahim Pasha, heir to Egypt, had to evacuate his troops, and Emir Bashir II, on October 13, 1840, was exiled to Malta, from where he was taken to Istanbul.

It is a convert of Austrian origin, Omar who replaces him, putting an end to the relative autonomy of Mount Lebanon.

Following the protest of the Great Powers to the Porte, the Lebanese entity, according to Metternich's plan, is divided into two "cantons", one north of the road to Beirut Damascus, made up of Metn and Kesrouan, Populated mostly by Christians, administered by a notable Maronite, the other, south of the road, populated mainly by Druze and administered by a notable Druze.

Gérard de Nerval, who stayed in Lebanon in 1843 deplores this situation insofar as "it separates the two components of the Mountain".

Troubles broke out in 1844 and 1845.

In 1846, the population of Mount Lebanon was estimated at 300,000 people, including 190,000 Maronites, 37,000 Greeks Catholics, 25,000 Greeks Orthodox, 32,000 Druze, 9,000 Sunnis and 9,800 Shiites.

In 1858, new massacres, initiated by the Ottomans mourn the mountain, and those of 1860, where 15,000 Christians perished as well in Mount Lebanon as in Damascus and Zahle, causing the reaction of the Great Powers.

From May 1860 to June 1861, an expeditionary force sent by Napoleon III occupied the Christian mountain, leading many Druze to expatriate in the south of Syria, the "Jebel Druze".

The Hamdan notables fled, but the Attrache family of Soueida eliminated them in 1869.

It is therefore an international intervention which arises for the second time in twenty years and imposes on the Turks a special status for Lebanon.

This "organic regulation" of Lebanon creates an Executive Council of 12 members (4 Maronites, 3 Druze, 2 Greek Orthodox, 1 Greek Catholic, 1 Sunni, 1 Shiite), chaired by a prefect (moutassaref), an Ottoman official, but necessarily Christian. of non-Lebanese origin.

This formula will last until the First World War.

In 1840, the Druze obtained an official community status ("Millet") instituting courts, mortmain property for religious establishments, education and a denominational aid service, which were their own.

Druze communities of the Near East in the 20th and early 21st centuries

Still few in number (their institutional monogamy penalizes them compared to Sunni or Shiite Muslims), the Druze are spread across neighboring countries hostile to each other, Lebanon and Syria, Syria and Israel.

Lebanon has 320,000 to 400,000, Syria 600,000, Israel 130,000, Jordan 20,000.

Their secret esoteric religion enables them to adopt a vigilant attitude of safeguard vis-à-vis the executive powers, which they reconcile with that of responsible citizens.

But considered by Sunnis as heretics, preferring to reside in Christian areas, devoid of mosques because they do not go there, they do not follow the five canonical Muslim obligations, and therefore are not called to testify before a "Sharia" court.

Economic exile hits them too; 100,000 Druze live in South America, which weakens them even more locally.

In the medium term, like the Yazidis of Iraq or Syria, they will be called upon to join a community of their choice or with their defending body more able to defend them collectively.

1- In Lebanon

It has been said "communities are anxious to use state apparatus ... Their roles may be different depending on circumstances and necessities and may change sides; a good example is the Druze community in the case of Lebanon "

Since independence, in fact, this is what the Druze community has done, especially in its relations with the Maronites.

Allied with the pro-Nasser Sunnis, in 1958, the Druze and their leaders played the card of alliance, if not fusion, with the Syrians even after the assassination of Kamal Joumblatt in 1977, for which the latter are responsible.

Today confronted with neighbors with galloping demography, the Shiites, they may regret having, during the events of 1958, 1975 and 1976, 1983, allowed the massacres of or participated in the execution of many Christians, leading to an exodus. massive 100,000 of them in Beirut.

This space emptied of its inhabitants attracts the desires of southern Lebanese, largely belonging to the Shiite community.
They no longer have their great leader, Kamal Joumblatt, a life deputy since the age of 25 and who, by founding the Progressive Socialist Party (PSP), tried to give his people a national audience that went beyond community recruitment. .

An international personality, as unpredictable in his role as Minister as he was as an opponent, he benefited from an exceptional charisma, which in another state less governed by confessionalism, would have led him to the Presidency of the Republic.

A Druzo-Maronite directorate of regional affairs, succeeded during the mandate a Maronito-Sunni alliance, which would like to replace by eliminating one of the two partners, the Shiite leadership, now at the head of the most numerous community (1 Lebanese in 3 is Shiite).

On April 30, 2001, Walid Joumblatt declared:

"It seems that for some Arab leaders, the minorities must join the majority ..."

These minorities have no value today in modern political science in vogue in the Arab world.
This seems all the more true as the Druze are still divided into two opposing clans, which today is called between Joumblatti and Yazbacki (the Arslan clan).

This tension further weakens the community.

The future of the Druze in Lebanon, as an autonomous Muslim faith, is in serious jeopardy.

The only national cultural unit that remains are the sanctuaries of the holy characters, frequented by Druze, Christians and Muslims like that of the Prophet Ayoub (Job) in the Shouf.
But it's very small.

2- In Syria

The Druze made up around 3% of Syria's pre-war population in 2011 (23 million people), or around 600,000 people.

Historical:

The Druze community is found mainly in the province of Soueida but also in pockets of the north-west and near the capital Damascus.

As in Mount Lebanon, with which there were many exchanges, the Druze rarely bowed to the centralism of the Ottoman Empire, refusing the incorporation of the imperial army.

In 1866, Chebli Bey Attrache led a revolt of the harshly suppressed Djebel Druze.

In 1910, the Turks killed the father of Sultan Attrache of Salkhad.

Thus, the Druze rallied to Emir Fayçal Hachem, in 1918, at the time of the proclamation of the Kingdom of Syria, whose Druze region, called the Emirate, of Jebel, was entrusted to Selim Pasha El Attrache on August 4, 1921.

When the French mandate was established in 1921, Paris also proclaimed the autonomy of the "state of Jebel Druze", with its 70,000 inhabitants.

This statute will remain in force from March 1922 to December 1936.

This did not prevent the Druze from revolting in 1925 with Sultan Pasha El Attrache; they will reoffend in 1937 and 1939.

In 1942, the "Jebel" was administratively attached to Damascus, and in 1944 the Jebel Administrative Council unanimously voted to repeal the special regime and its incorporation into the Syrian state.

From 1926 to 1945, the balances of the cavalrymen of the Druze proxy squadrons had brought an appreciable improvement.

In 1947, 100,000 Druze lived in Syria, 90% of them Jebel Druze, the rest residing in a southwestern suburb of Damascus, Germana, and in the southwestern suburb of Aleppo.

A few hundred workers are working, on a temporary basis, in Palestine, in the salt mines of the Dead Sea.

The young Syrian Republic will have a problem with them.

President Kouatly, in 1947, will try to encourage the peasants to fight against the large traditional owners, then President Chichakli will suppress the revolt of 1954 by air force.

Overthrown by a coup, and a refugee in Brazil, he was assassinated there by a Druze.

The Druze officers of the Syrian army will benefit from accelerated advancements as to assert themselves over the Sunnis, the Alawis will rely on their Ismaili and Druze partners.

Thus, in 1962, General Zahreddine would be promoted to Commander-in-Chief, but very quickly the split between the anti-Sunnis would occur; Baath cadres Colonel Salim Hatoum and Talal Abi Assli will oppose Alawite Salam Jedid and Ismaili Abdel Karim Jundi.

They will be executed.

However, at the funeral of Sultan Attrache in 1982, President Hafez el Assad and a million of his compatriots will be present.

If in the cultural field (the President of the Syrian Writers Union, Ali Oqla Arsan, was Druze), the "Unitarists" are respected, it is no longer the same in the political field.
The solidarity of esoteric minorities ("Batiniyyin", ie Ismailis, Druze, Alaouites) is no longer on the agenda.

It is that the Alawis have developed a policy of mixed marriages with the families of Sunni notables, rich and famous, delighted to unite in power.

The Druze are no longer able to do so and become marginalized contenders.

However careful to maintain an appearance of Islam, they protest if it is challenged.

In 1991, the daily "Al Ahram" published a "Fatwa" stating that Druzism was not at all Islamic.

Supreme Sheikh Aql Jarjoura complained to President Mubarak, who replied:

"The Fatwa dated back to 1936 and had not been reactivated by the Grand Mufti of Egypt, Sheikh Tantawi."

For the sake of deconfessionalization, the Syrian authorities changed the name from "Djebel Druze" to "Arab Djebel", then today to "Province of Soueida" as had been done for the "Mountain of the Alaouites" or the "Valley". Christians ".

Clashes (in 2001) between Druze and nomadic Arabs took place in the vicinity of Soueida over grazing issues, but the Sunnis, to have the good role claimed that they wanted this land to build a mosque.

Supreme Sheikh Akl Druze telephoned President Bashar al-Assad who reassured him and had these problems resolved for the benefit of the Druze, and without the intervention of the local governor (non-Druze), thus perpetuating the political and confessional function of the highest authority. Syrian Druze nun.

This denominational reference to obtaining appeasement of a social conflict in a sensitive region is symptomatic of the way in which the Druze community is still perceived by the public authorities.

The Syrian Druze community became divided with the popular uprising in 2011 against the regime of Bashar al-Assad.

At the start of the revolt, one of the first soldiers to defect from the army was Officer Druze Khaldoun Zeinedinne, who died in clashes with regime forces.

Others have remained loyal, such as General Issam Zahreddine, one of the army's top Druze officers, who died in 2017 in a mine explosion after fighting against ISIS.

The community leaders, by adopting a cautious attitude towards the regime, sought to preserve some independence in their regions and to protect themselves from a possible offensive from Damascus.

Sheikh Wahid al-Balous, a religious dignitary who denounced both the regime and jihadist groups, symbolizes this policy of distancing.

Killed in an attack in Soueida in 2015, he had opposed the sending of army conscripts from Soueida to fight outside the province.

In the province of Soueida, the Druze created armed militias.

The most powerful, that of the "Sheikhs of Dignity", led by Sheikh Balous until his death, fought fierce battles against ISIS and the Syrian branch of Al Qaeda.

Other groups were linked to the regime, including Dareh al-Watan (Shield of the Fatherland), a militia founded in April 2015 with 2,000 combatants strong.

3- In Israel

From their flight from Egypt in the 11th century, a number of Druze settled in Galilee, which was, in the 16th century, partly conquered by Emir Fakhreddin.

This community took root, and was repeatedly described by 19th century European travelers.

In 1948, sixteen villages of Galilee and two of Mount Carmel were inhabited by Druze and Christians.

During the 1948 war, some Druze supported the creation of the State of Israel, others refused to take sides.

Today, the Druze, considered as a "non-Arab" minority, are the only non-Jewish Israeli citizens (with a few Muslim nomads) to benefit from social advantages (free healthcare, access to social housing), and to perform military service in the "Tsahal" (Israeli army), which puts them in the face of hostility from the Palestinians.

However, their status is sometimes endangered as a result of successive Israeli wars.

So in 1967, when the Golan was annexed, Arabs and Circassians abandoned their villages, while six thousand Druze remained, some pro Israel, others pro-Syrians.

In 1973, the Israeli government wanted to impose an Israeli identity card on them and only 400 Druze accepted it.

In 1980, the Likud government renewed the pressure, and it was thanks to the Druze of Galilee that Bégin once again had to give up the plan for the general naturalization of the Druze of the Golan.

In 1983, during the invasion of Lebanon, the Druze soldiers of the IDF refused to go and fight their Lebanese co-religionists, especially since the Israelis openly supported the Christian community.

Israeli Druze actively participated in negotiations between the Druze militias in Lebanon and the Israeli army.

This mediation will cause the Israeli government to abandon the Christians of Lebanon to their fate, hence the massacres that followed.

The first Druze (Arab) Likud MP, Nasreddine, in 1983 summed up the attitude of his community in Israel:

"The Druze Unit exists, but we are loyal to our respective countries."

This "citizen" integration is illustrated by the access to employment of the Druze in the Israeli civil service: the army, the police, the parallel services, the prison guards.

It is in Israel that Druze culture and religion seem destined for public debate, as in the United States.

The writer Druze Mosbah Halabi, originally from the village of Carmel, described in his novel "Diary of a Druze Girl (1991)" the beliefs kept secret (including reincarnation) and reserved for initiates.

500 copies of the book were publicly burned in the Druze region, and the author was the object of a sort of major excommunication which left him indifferent, since he was uninitiated.

Moreover, the free contacts between young Druze and young Israelis are pushing more and more Israeli Druze citizens to demand clarifications on their religion of which they have always been deprived.

4 - In the Diaspora

In today's diaspora, how can the young Druze remain attached to their customs, when there is no longer any community supervision abroad?

Perhaps the solution will come from the United States; expatriate members of the Druzo-American Association have started to speak openly about their faith, their rite, which only 20% of initiates are allowed to follow.

So what is the Druze religion for the uninitiated?

The past has kept the community in accepted ignorance, but the future will demand that this question be answered.

Two generally shared elements of analysis apply to the Druze of distant emigration (Europe, America, Australia).

The first is that the socio-cultural conditions of expatriates reproduce the usual strata of Druze communities in countries of origin (Lebanon, Syria, Israel).

The second is the emergence of a more educated Druze society that requires its initiates to be more in tune with the modern world as well.

To fully understand why the Druze do not experience difficulties in maintaining their culture in expatriation, it must be borne in mind that they form a "Muslim community" according to the five pillars of orthodox Islam, interpreted, he is true, in a sense that is not literal and which is described in the following chapters.
The presence of a clergy is therefore not essential.

Living a Druze life does not require a Druze environment.

As only 10 to 15% of the Druze population can be initiated, the Diaspora does not change much.

A Druze can go to a mosque or a church, pray there, follow the ceremonies there, provided that he remains inside Druze; when he wakes up, before taking his meals, he has at his disposal the recitation of formulas which keep him in his faith.

On the other hand, to listen to lectures from educated Druze, one does not need to be initiated.

Thus the community adopts political or communications measures to maintain the presence of socio-cultural networks of the countries of origin in those of the diaspora.

The creation of a Council for expatriate Druze, set up by Walid Joumblatt and Marwan Hamadé, was prohibited by the Syrian government.

The Ourfan Institute in Beirut has therefore created a website to answer questions from expatriates and disseminate religious teachings.

Regional cultural centers abroad have been opened.

In England in Oxford, the "British Druze Society" and in France "the French Druze Association".

In Africa in Nigeria "the Nigerian Druze Commitee".

In Latin America:

- In Venezuela "the Venezuelan Cultural Druze Society".

- In Brazil in Sao Paulo "the Druze Center".

- In Argentina in Buenos Aires "the Druze Charity Association".

- In Mexico in Mexico City "the Druze Commitee".

In Australia in Melbourne where the headquarters of the Australian Druze

Association of Victoria are located and in Sydney that of the Australian Druze Association of New South Wales.

The Druze are well represented in the United States and Canada, which are probably home to the largest groups.

In Canada in Toronto is the headquarters "The Canadian Druze Society" with branches in Montreal "La Druze Association of Montreal" and in Edmonton "the Druze Association of Edmonton".

In the United States, the first Druze organization, "El Bakaurat Ed Dirziyat", was founded by immigrants in 1908 in Seattle, Washington.

Over the years, the latter had given ten branches across the country until the last ceased all activity in 1964.

In the meantime, and to meet the needs of a community, no longer composed only of immigrants but also of people born in the United States, the American Druze Society was created in 1947 in Charleston, Virginia.

His goals were complementary to "El Bakaurat Ed Dirziyat".

The American Druze Society obtained, in 1977, that the American administration exempt it from taxes and that the donations which are paid to it are deductible.

Every year, this Association organizes a Convention which takes place in principle in the United States, also abroad, thus proving its desire to maintain the unity of the entire Druze community throughout the world.

In 1973, for the first time, a Convention was held abroad, in Beirut.

On this occasion, the organization's leaders visited the leaders of the Lebanese Druze community, Kamal Joumblatt and Emir Magid Arslan.

The civil war prevented the experience from being repeated.

The second Convention organized abroad took place in Canada, in Toronto in 1980.

Since 1982, there has been a Druze lobby in Washington made up of members of the American Druze Society, the American Druze Society Affairs Committee (ADPAC).

This has set itself the objective of informing the public and the media about the Druze reality in the United States.

In addition, the American Druze Society of San Francisco has 25 Sheikhs, responsible for going to the "Khalwa" to initiate or "Majlis", or prayers are said on Thursday evening.

Likewise, in Los Angeles, the Institute of Druze Studies disseminates cultural concepts and historical studies.

But this openness to the outside, this insertion of young Druze into very different modern societies has led officials to re-examine the function of missionaries and the role abroad of places of gathering, the "Majlis".

They noted that there was a lack, from a historical point of view, of works dating from the early days of Druzism, and which could explain the appearance of this community, and from a strictly ceremonial point of view that the ritualism of the initiates, moreover often men of virtue, no longer won the support of young intellectuals.

It is that initiation is not a transferable experience, which could be transcribed through scientific textbooks.

It is, for everyone, an inner subjective experience, which does not transform the individual into a religious official (mufti, imam) or a "monk".

This is a direct relationship with God, as known to the Sufis; Druzism is therefore closely linked to Islam and the Koran.

Moreover, at the beginning, the "Da'wa" (pastoral) was a "Ta'wil", a second-degree commentary on the Qur'an, vivified by the presence of the Imam.

This non-dogmatic attitude is subject to persecution, like Hallaj, by supporters of official politico-religious conservatism.

We thus came to the realization that the separation no longer takes place between initiates and uninitiated in expatriate Druze society, but between educated and uneducated individuals, because being initiated does not necessarily mean being educated.

From where, to reconstitute a community unit, to appeal to candidates having a good university training, the knowledge of a prolonged insertion in a non-Druze environment, in fact being an initiate, but educated in secular sciences, of the dangers of globalization , because religion would no longer be accepted as dogma, but as proof.

Hence, this Druze renewal movement called "neomouwahidism" and which is based on the deepening of philosophical knowledge and the foundations of modern humanism.

The other observation is that in fact few Druze know the teachings of philosophy, as the rule of life of an existence unfolding on two planes, spiritual and material.

Kamal Joumblatt had insisted on the precepts of Hindu philosophy, as the key to the perfect city.

In Druze teaching, the great Greek philosophers are revered, as much Plato, who influenced the works of Al Ghazali, Ibn Maskaweih, Ibn Hazm, as Aristotle one of the sources of "Tawheed".
Logic shows that God created man free; it is up to him to seek harmony between his roots and his daily life.

The philosophy, for the Druze, lies in the adjustment of exterior and interior behavior.

Adjustment with modern humanism, which the new community elite defines as interprofessional, intercultural, intercultural dialogue.

Thanks to the contribution of young educated and liberal Druze immigrants, religion becomes an education, the science of "Tawheed" opening up to new technologies.

Chapter II

A Syncretic Doctrine

Bahaedinne el Muqtana, contemporary of Caliph Al Hakim defined the Druze Doctrine as follows:

"The Doctrine of the Unity of the Lord (Tawheed) is the fruit of all the religions that have existed in the past centuries:
It is the balance of equity by which the earth and the heavens subsist ".

And for the initiate Kamal Joumblatt:

"It is a religion of meditators, a religion which, like the ancient Greek philosophy, gave meaning to life, to society and to human destiny.

Aristotle, one of our sages, doesn't he say somewhere that the goal of life is meditation on Reason.

It is not a religion like any other, a Shari'a (Law) in the Koranic or Hebrew sense of the term, nor a religion based on faith like Christianity or Islam.

For the Druze, what is important is inner conviction, it is "seeing", it is realizing inner truth, knowledge of the self, the "mental" stripping of everything in order to know the absolute.

It is a religion of spiritual ascetics, of Gnostics practicing life; a religion of ethics as much as of knowledge.

The "know thyself" from which the spirit of truth stems is one of its foundations, hence the essential research pursued by the Druze: total authenticity ".

- History:

The elaboration of this Doctrine was carried out from One hundred and Eleven Epistles collected in Six Books, known collectively under the title of "Book of Wisdom".

The first thirty-five epistles are attributed to Hamza Ibn Ali, the epistles 36 to 40 to Ismail el Tamimi, and the epistles 41 to 111 to Bahaedinne el Muqtana.

We know the date of the writing of the Sixth (01 July 1017) and the Hundred Ninth and Hundred Tenth (1042).

It was much later that from this corpus, the Druze theologians would write the laws and moral rules, the foundations of Druzism.

They are Sayid Jamaleddin el Tanoukhi (1417-1479), jurisconsult and Sufi, having lived in Aban (Lebanon), Sheikh Zeyneddine Abdeljaafar Takieddine, from Baakline (Lebanon), who died in 1557, and the great Aql Sheikhs of the 18th century century of origin of Chouf or Wadi el Taym, on the Syrian-Lebanese border.

Another esoteric work is supposed to disclose an initiatory teaching in the Druze movement, it is the "Book of Points and Circles".

These texts will be gradually translated into French first insofar as a Greek Orthodox doctor from Damascus Nasrallah Ibn Gilde in 1700 offered King Louis XIV three Druze books.

It was the orientalist Venture de Paradis who was the first to undertake a study of the Druze doctrine, in the middle of the 18th century, with other manuscripts having been brought back to France.

In the 19th century, Sylvestre de Sacy, director of the School of Oriental Languages in Paris and Henri Guys, French consul in Beirut, will devote books to Druzism that Gérard de Nerval will consult, who will be inspired by it in his "Voyage en Orient". .

Since El Tanoukhi, no communication has been made to the Druze public outside of the initiation circles, which required learning the doctrine over a large number of years.

This is why the translation of the Druze books did not seem embarrassing to theologians, because, they said, the symbolic meaning of the texts remained incomprehensible to the uninitiated.

- A hierarchical Divine Order

Applying Hermes theory:

"What is above is like what is below and vice versa", esotericists, Shiites, Ismailis, Alawites, Druze, or "Batiniyyin" believe that like earthly society, celestial beings are classified hierarchically according to the principle:

"God also has his god".
This, moreover, is linked to "Tawhid", that is to say to the dogma of divine Oneness to which all Muslims, whether Sunni or Shiite, are attached and

which they summarize in the statement:

"There is no god but God".
To show their attachment to Orthodox Sunni doctrine, the Druze do the same but imply that "Tawheed" means the union of humanity with the divine nature; thus to access "Tawheed" is to understand that the oneness of beings resides in God, who can, at certain times, appear in the world of men to help them and thus affirm the Oneness.

In the spirit of the Druze, God, at the origin of the three successive monotheisms, created "Druzism", to unify the successive dogmas revealed at the creation of each religion.

That is why they are called among themselves "Mouwahidoun", the "Unitarians".

All that exists is by Divine Intelligence, called AQL.

God is not above the world. He is in the world. It is a pantheistic conception.

Nevertheless, Druzism seems to take from Manichaeism its conceptions of the creation of evil through pride, and this as we move away from Pancreator.

Universal Intelligence, also called the Highest Reason, created all souls by its single emanation, as well as all dogmas and truths of religion.
Then the Divine Intelligence AQL, becomes aware of its own perfection and constitutes itself as a separate entity, because it is by becoming aware of a perfection distinct from God that the AQL separates itself from God.

So, disobedience is created from obedience, darkness from light, ignorance from wise-knowledge.

Satan, the entity of evil, the Adversary, as the Druze call him, strengthens himself with the awareness of his personal perfection.

Evil is therefore constituted within even the highest instances of Good.

To help fight the Adversary, at the request of the AQL, God creates the Soul (the NAFS).

The NAFS becomes the activity of the Will of God, but in turn, the Soul will engender a rival entity which will take Satan's side, this is the "NIDD".

In any case, the Soul takes the role of a woman with regard to the Intelligence which takes the role of the male; inferior to Intelligence, it is placed immediately after the latter above all other Beings.

So, NAFS feels the need to create another entity that will bring it closer to God, and that is the Word (KALIMA), an indispensable tool of reasoning and thought, and vital principle.

To help the Word in the world of appearances, a fourth entity, after the AQL, the KALIMA, is created; it is about the Perfection of Cosmic Beings (Al SABEQ, that is to say the one who is at the head); this fourth entity receives help from a fifth, the Perfection of Bodily Beings (Al TALI, that is, the one that follows).

The Previous is considered to be the source of harmony and order for the Universe, and the Next is the expression of the perfection of bodily beings.

The bodily world, it has been understood, is the result of an interaction between the good which attracts man to God, and the evil which is concerned with distinguishing itself from others by material advantages.

To defend himself, a man must then be convinced that:

- God is the author of all being.

- the Will of God, AQL, is the cause of all cosmic principles.

- cosmic principles are the source of all material existence.

The "Rival" principle of Evil in the world is often referred to (biblical loan?) As the Calf; to serve one's interests is to sacrifice to the "Cult of the Calf".

The uninitiated equate the doctrine of the "evil eye" with the "servants of the Calf", although this is disapproved of by the Sages.

Just as all souls incarnate continuously, the greater entities do so at periods defined by cycles, and when AQL incarnates in an individual of flesh, the Word (KALIMA) incarnates at the same time in another, as well as the two Perfections (Al SABEQ and Al TALI).

The first incarnation of the AQL will have been CHATTNIL, who is not the ADAM of the Bible and the Koran, but the spiritual father of humanity from the first times, and who was betrayed by his two assistants, ADAM, and EVE, who was not a woman, but the spiritual receptacle of Gnosis.

Then Jethro (CHOUEÏB) will embody the AQL in the time of Moses, Lazare in the time of Jesus, Salman al Farisi in the time of Mohammed.

In each era there is embodied an exoteric envoy, the NATIQ, in charge of liturgical revelation and the ASSAS, esoteric envoy, who will consolidate the tradition from within.

We will thus have NOE and SHEM, ABRAHAM and ISMAEL, MOISE and ARON, JESUS and PIERRE, MOHAMMED and ALI.

These successive incarnations of initiates at the highest level, the "IMAMS", will allow the Druze to study, progressively, all the successive messages of faith.

This divine pentad will also be embodied around Caliph Al Hakim:

- **Hamza**, born in Iran as we have seen on the same date as Al Hakim, will be the **embodiment of Intelligence.**

- His son-in-law **Ismail Al Tamimi** that of the **Soul**

- Abu Abdallah Mohamed Ibn Wahab **Al Qorachi** that of the **Word**

- Abulkhair **as-Samini** that of the **Previous**

and

Bahaeddine Al Moqtana, disciple of Hamza, that of the **Next**.

It was the latter who made the decision to stop all proselytism in 1043.

To this conception of the permanent Reincarnation of Celestial Entities is added that of the end of the world.

The latter is lived, like the great monotheisms like the day of judgment.

Each soul will be judged according to the lives it has led.

Almighty God will annihilate his enemies, chastise the followers of ungodly religions and make the Druze triumph.

On that day, all dogmas and false religions will disappear, leaving room only for the Druze, forever.

- An embodied human hierarchy

The Druze Cosmogony unfolds in a cyclical conception of time.

Since the primordial Manifestation, seven cycles have unfolded, oscillating between periods of mankind's progress towards the Truth "Haqq" and of ebb into ignorance ("Jahiliyya").

Our time is part of the 7th cycle, which has known 6 eras of prophecy: those of Noah, Abraham, Moses, Jesus, Mohammed and Ismail Abu Mohammed, before the advent of Al Hakim, the ultimate manifestation of the divinity, with whom the truth was totally revealed.

At the top of the hierarchy, these "exoteric" prophets are holders of a particle of divine power, while their esoteric "doubles" support them, in the order: Shem, Ishmael, Aron, Peter, Ali.

Below them, preachers are responsible for spreading the divine message, as are evangelists for Christ.

Other beings propagate the doctrine of the imamate, or initiate neophytes, or even introduce doubt into the minds of those who seek the truth in order to make them more aware.

At the level of religious frameworks, the forces of darkness can also be embodied, for the spiritual life is a constant struggle against the surrounding Evil.

In order to protect themselves, the uninitiated have at their disposal seven mandatory precepts to follow, which are:

1- not to lie (therefore not to steal, not to kill, not to be adulterous),

2- love his brothers in faith and come to their aid,

3- not believing "in your soul" in other religions,

4- not to reveal the mysteries of our Lord,

5- renounce the "Rival"

6- be subject to the divine will,

7- be strong and resigned to happiness as well as to adversity
Alongside these precepts of obligation, there are those called "invitation": to be humble and charitable, not to drink wine, to avoid lust.

Finally, male circumcision is recommended only from a hygienic point of view.

It goes without saying that there is a close solidarity between the Druze among themselves, who must constantly and sincerely help each other.

- Metempsychosis and Taquiyya

Druze eschatology is very different from Muslim or Christian eschatology which considers that man has only one life on earth.

The Druze believe in Metempsychosis = Taqammus.

They believe that souls are born once and for all.
When bodily existence has had its day, the soul is reincarnated in the body of a child who has just been born.

This is valid for all mankind, except that a Druze soul can only reincarnate in a Druze body.

This body can only be human and therefore not in animals.

The proof of metempsychosis would be in the "mind" of the man who has amassed in him memories, knowledge and knowledge during his previous lives.

A Druze never says he dies; he says he is transmigrating.

Here is how Kamal Joumblatt defined it:

"We believe that after death the soul immediately settles into an unborn baby and enters the flesh through the breath.

In his mother's womb, the child had hitherto only lived in an animal way; It is only at the moment when it begins to breathe that the soul settles there its abode.

The Rosicrucians, on the other hand, believe that the soul can remain for a certain time in a larval or etheric state before passing into another body, and that there is a certain latency between death and the new birth ".

At the base of their beliefs, the Druze placed faith in the immortality of the soul and in its reincarnation in several bodies, until the times when, having become completely pure, it will forever melt "in the light and in joy".

This union with the divinity will moreover be achieved only to varying degrees, and each one will be able to "see" God only in the proportion of the good acts which he will have accomplished during his successive reincarnations.

"To reach higher existences, you, Druze, you must possess the Druze spirit and all the virtues that" the Highest Reason "teaches you: because, for the eternal and true life of your soul, your present life does not is only one day.

It has been preceded by an infinite number of previous lives, and will be followed by similar lives, until the day when your mind has become infinitely pure, Hakim's eyes will be able to fix on you and attract you ".

In order to protect themselves from the outside world and from the majority religions, the Druze can defend themselves by **"Taquiyya"**, or concealment of their faith (it consists of hiding their belief in a non-Druze context), if necessary by adopting the main or national religion (especially Sunni Islam), at least outside, because the Druze do not fast during Ramadan (initiates do so under other conditions), they do not follow any Muslim ceremony, apart from Ashura (commemoration of the assassination of the Prophet's grandson by the Sunnis), which is celebrated by the Shiites; as regards the "Sharia", they have a code of special laws within the framework of the Druze Courts, in particular for the equality of men and women (polygamy prohibited, divorce for the benefit of the wife, independence of the patrimony of the wife).

Objects of all persecutions, the Druze must protect their beliefs against any distortion that popularization would imply and against the hatred that their particularism could arouse.

The Druze can, for example, pray in a Church or a Mosque, without his Druze faith being called into question.

- Lahut and Nasut

Hamza in his 7th Epistle conceives of Lahut and Nasut as follows:

"Our Lord reveals himself to his creatures in a form similar to theirs, having taken the appearance of one of his creatures, so that men may partly grasp the power of his rank (Maqâm) and hear his words emanating from human nature (Nasut) of the form he has put on.
As for the divinity (Lahut) of Our Lord and the true nature of his essence, he is the Causator of the cause of causes, the Old, the Eternal, imperceptible to the imagination, incomprehensible to the intelligence, impermeable to thought and representation, not likely to be dispersed or reunited, and very high above what they describe ".

The meaning of Divinity (Al Lahut) and Humanity (Al Nasut):

Lahutia (Divinity), expresses that which is Divine by its Existence and access to its Knowledge.

While Nasutia, means the process of Human Anthropomorphy by its Existence and its Gnostic Mysticism

Since God, according to TAWHID DRUZE is the ONE and the Only ABSOLUTE without any specific Attribute, His Divinity (Lahut) therefore cannot, in any case, be Intelligent by Human (Nasut), which, whose specificity is "Being = Al Zatia".

Hence the Human (Nasut), despite all the degrees of his elevation towards Perfection, can perceive of the Divine (Lahut) only what his degree of his Human Transcendence allows him.

That is to say, what allows him, his limited possibility, to perceive God through Gnostic and Transcendental Mysticism.

The Absolute Principle (God), did not Create the Universe, including Man, Ex-Nihilo (but Ab Initio), because this concept (Interior and Exterior = Ex-Nihilo), gives the appearance of Limits to the Creator-God.

But "AL ABDA-A" created Man (and the Universe) in an INCOMPARABLE way (AL IBDA-Â).

That is, He Intelligent Him with His Own Light, by Absolute Appearance, for it is His own Intellectual Nature (Al Izhar).

The Universe, of which Man is a part, is the Obligatory Translation of God (= His Theophanic Manifestation).

Hence, Creation in the sense of making the Universe (Being) Ex Nihilo exist, out of DIVINE LIGHT, is in contradiction with the Absolute Creator Principle, and makes Divine Quiddity limited.

Also, to affirm this, is a non-Unique-Unifying process, and contrary to Divine Unity, because it necessarily leads to a DUALITY:

That of God and that of the Universe.

This is in complete contradiction to TAWHID, or Divine Oneness.

Therefore, Tawheed does not believe in the Existence of Two separate Worlds: World of God and World of Man, or Heaven and Earth, the World of Immanence and the Eschatological World.

Therefore, he does not believe that God is somewhere and that Man is elsewhere.

The Absolute Principle = God, is out of Time (Chronos) and Space (Being-Place).

We can also say that God "is not" (verb to be) everywhere, but every Physical Place is in Him, without saying that it means a Place.

Hence the Mouwahidoun (Unitarists), say that Humanity (in the sense of Man) Theophanic (Al Nasutia), is not separate or distinct from Divinity.

For Man is to Divinity what (Creative) Sense is to Word, and which is the Expression of Divinity.

And since the Absolute Divinity is limitless, His Human Manifestation, indeed, is not external to his own Existence, but is his Expression (Spiritual Materialization).

The binding of the Word (Creator), which has its own Meaning

(Materialization of the Word), does not mean that Scripture (as a Non-Symbolic figure) is His Expression.

The same is true of the Universe, which, despite expressing God, and being related to him, is not God Himself.

He is related through His Emanation and He is distinct through His own Truth of Existence (Quiddity of Divine Existence).

Hence Heaven is on "Earth" (Immanent Existence) and not in "Heaven", for there is no Heaven separate from Earth.

Hence the Druze (Monotheistic) Unitary Way calls for liberation from Duality, that is, from the Belief that Existence is Dual (Dichotomous):

Celestial Existence and Terrestrial Existence, or Good and bad Existence.

The Unitarian Mystic Druze thinks that the evil World is the one, which the Adept causes to be separated from Eternity; whereas the Immanent World, not separated by the Adept from Eternity, makes the latter a Good and True Eternity.
The Immanent World is destruction, if it is not the Expression of Eternity.

If Man believes that he is the Theophany of his Creator, and therefore exists by his Humanitude in God, not as an Individual, or even less as an Entity devoid of Divinity, then he becomes Mouwahhid (Having Faith in Divine Oneness).

But if the Adept believes that God (Creator Principle) has a particular Quiddity, and that he created him Ex Nihilo, independently of time and Places (Space), ruling him as a simple creature, then this adept " worship "God for fear of" Hell ", or in the Hope of Heaven.

Submission to God is not that, but rather that of his Prostration (Adoration = Contemplation), so that he can REALIZE himself in GOD.

- The Catechism of the Druze (followed by explanations and comments)

This catechism, which must have been written in the 18th century in the Syro-Lebanese region according to the model of Christian catechisms, is addressed to "Johhâl" (ignorant) so that they know their religion thoroughly.

Q: Are you Druze?

A: I am, thanks to our almighty Lord.

Q: What is a Druze?

A: He is the one who wrote down the law and worships the Creator.

Q: What did the Creator command you?

A: To be truthful, to abide by His worship and to observe the seven conditions.

Q: What difficult duties has your Lord exempted you from and how do you know that you are truly Druze?

A: I do what is lawful and I refrain from what is illegal.

Q: What is lawful and illegal?

A: What belongs to the priesthood and to agriculture is lawful. What belongs to temporal places and renegades is illegal.

Q: Under what conditions did our almighty Lord manifest himself?

A: He manifested in the year 400 of the Hegira of Muhammad and he declared himself of the race of Muhammad to hide his divinity.

Q: Why did he have to hide his divinity?

A: Because his cult was neglected and few worshiped him.

Q: When did he manifest his divinity?

A: In the year 408 of the Hegira of Muhammad.

Q: How long has he been doing it?

A: Throughout the year 408 of the Hegira of Muhammad. Then he disappeared during the year 409 which was a bad year, but at the beginning of the year 410 he reappeared and remained throughout the year 411. He disappeared at the beginning of the year 412 of the Hegira of Muhammad. He will not reappear until the day of judgment.

Q: What is the day of judgment?

A: It is the one where the Creator will appear with a human figure and where he will rule the universe by power and the sword (1)

Q: When will this take place?

A: We don't know, but there will be warning signs.

Q: What signs?

A: We will see kings change and Christians have the advantage over Muslims.

Q: What month is this going to happen?

A: In the moon of Jamadi Awal or in the moon of Rajab, according to the calculations of the Hegira.

Q: How will God react to people and leaders?

A: He will manifest himself by the power of the sword and he will take the life of everyone.

Q: What will happen then after their death?

A: They will be reborn at the command of the Almighty and they will do what he wills.

Q: How will he deal with them?

A: He will separate them into four groups: Christians, Jews, Renegades (2).

Q: How will each of these groups divide?

A: The Christians who are the Noseïris (Nazarenes) and the Metwalis (Shiites); the Jews and the Renegades who turned away from the religion of our Lord El Hakim.

Q: What will God do to the faithful in his unit?

A: He will grant them empire, royalty, property, gold and silver. They will dwell in the world and be leaders.

Q: What will happen to the renegades?

A: They will be excruciatingly punished. When they are hungry and thirsty, their food will become bitter. They will be burdened with the hardest work in the true worshipers of God. Jews and sectarian Christians will experience similar but less harsh punishments.

Q: How many times has the Lord taken on a human appearance?

A: Ten times, called Maqâmat (Stations), in the singular Maqâm, it is the human person in which God manifests himself and reveals his divinity (Incarnation). It is also called "Veil", because God veils in it with his divinity.): He was successively called El-Aliy, El Bâr, Aliya, El-Mou'il, Abou Zakaria, El Qaïm, El Mansour, El Mu'izz, El Aziz and El Hakim (3).

Q: Where did the El Aliy station take place?

A: In India, in a town known as Jim Matchin (4).

Q: And El Bâr, where did he manifest himself?

A: In Persia, in a city called Isfahan. This is why the Persians say "Bâr-Khodâï"; Aliya manifested in Yemen; El-Mou'il in Morocco, in the form of a man who led a thousand camels; El Qaïm, also in Morocco, in a town called El-Mahdya. From there he came to Egypt where he manifested his divinity and built a port called El-Râchida. Abu Zakaria, El Mu'izz, El Aziz, El Mansour, and El Hakim all manifested in Egypt. El Mansour was called Ismaël.

Q: How many times has Hamza appeared and what were his names?

A: He appeared 7 times from Adam to Prophet Muhammad. In Adam's day his name was Chattnil; to that of Noah, his name was Pythagoras; to that of Abraham, his name was David; Chaïb was his name at the time of Moses; in Jesus' time, his name was the True Messiah and his name was Eleazar (Lazarus); in Muhammad's time he was called Salman el Farsi and in Said's time he was called Saleh (5).

Q: Where does the name Druze come from?

A: The name "Druze" comes from our obedience to the Hakim, as God wills and Hakim is our our Master Mohammed bin Ishmael (this is Nachtakine El Darazi) who manifested himself by himself to himself. .

When he manifested himself, the Druze followed his orders.

They "entered" into the law, which gave them the name of Druze.

Indeed, the Arabic term indarazna, yandarizu, darzan which means that they inserted themselves in it.

This therefore means that the Druze wrote the law, that he penetrated it and entered into the obedience of Hakim.

There is another etymology if we write Druze with an S (Druse), because it then derives from daras, iadros, which means to study.

So the Druze studied the books of Hamza and worshiped God appropriately.

Q: What does it mean: Our women swear by the "Yâkh" and our men by the "Wâh"?
A: Women use a feminine name and men use a masculine name.

The "Yâkh" means both "no and yes", as if one said: "no, my brother; Yes my brother".
It is the same when they say: "ay-wah" (yes or no).

Q: Why do we worship the gospel?

A: We want to pay homage to the name of the One who exists by order of God (Qaim b. Amrillah) and this is Hamza.

He was the one who spoke in the gospel.

In addition, it is appropriate that in the eyes of each nation we recognize their belief.
Moreover, if we worship the gospel, it is because this Book is based on divine wisdom and because it contains the obvious trace of true worship.

Q: Why do we reject any other book besides the Quran?

A: Because we are not to be recognized for who we are while we are among Muhammad's followers to be persecuted.

We have thus adopted all Muslim ceremonies, even prayers for the dead, all of this only outside, so that we can be ignored (6).

Q: What do we think of the "martyrs" whose courage and numbers Christians praise?
A: We claim that Hamza did not recognize them, even though all historians claim otherwise.

Q: What should we say then if Christians assure us that their faith cannot be questioned and that it is based on more valid evidence than Hamza's word? How then did we recognize that Hamza is infallible and that he is the pillar of truth of our salvation?

A: We can, by the testimony that Hamza gave himself.

He has indeed declared, in the Letter "Warnings and Exhortations":

"I am the first of God's creatures. I am his voice and his fist. I have science by his order. I am the tower and the built house. I am the master of death and resurrection. I am the one who will sound the trumpet. I am the supreme head of the priesthood, the master of grace, the builder and the destroyer of justice. I am the king of the world and the destroyer of the two testimonies. I am the fire that devours ".

Q: What is the true religion of the Druze?

A: It is the opposite of the beliefs of other nations. As it says in "The Epistle of Deception and Warning":

"Everything that others consider ungodly we admit and believe."

Q: If anyone came to know, believe and abide by our sacred tradition, would they be saved?
A: No the door is closed, the case is over, the pen is dull. After his death, his soul returns to his own nation and to his first religion.

Q: When were souls created?
A: They were after the creation of "Universal Reason" (the "Akl") which is

Hamza b.Ali. After him, God created the light, all the spirits which are numbered and which will neither decrease nor increase until the end of time.

Q: Is it appropriate for women to be initiated into the secrets of the Unitarian religion?

A: Yes, because our Lord imposed the pact on women too; they obeyed and followed the call of El-Hakim as it is mentioned in the Epistle "The Covenant of Women" and in "The Epistle to the Daughters".

Q: What should we think of other nations who claim to worship the Lord who created heaven and earth?

A: Even if they say this, their testimony is not true, because worship cannot be true without knowledge.

If they say: "We worship" without knowing that the Lord is El Hakim himself, their worship is false (7).

Q: Who, of the Ministers (Hudud) wrote the Epistles (of Wisdom) on which our religion is based?

A: Three Ministers wrote them; namely: Hamza, Ismaël and Bahaeddine.

Q: How many parts does science have?

A: Five

Two belong to religion and two others to nature.

The fifth, the most important of all, does not divide.
It is the true science, that of love and of God.

Q: How can we recognize that someone is our brother, a follower of true science if, coming to us, he declares himself Druze?

A: Here are the words of gratitude:

After the usual greetings, we must say:

"Are seeds of Myrobolan (Aliledji) sown in your country?" .

He must answer:

"Yes, it is sown in the hearts of believers".

So we have to ask him about our doctrine and whether he knows the "Ministers".

If he answers positively, he is our brother; otherwise he's just a stranger. (8)
Q: Who are the Ministers?

A: They are the prophets of El Hakim: Hamza, Ishmael, Muhammad, Abu El-Kheir and Bahaeddine (9).

Q: Do ignorant Druze have "salvation" or access to Hakim when they die in this state of ignorance?

A: There is no salvation for them and they will be in dishonor and slavery with our Lord until the eternity of eternities (reincarnation).

Q: Who is Doumassa? (10)

A: It is Adam the partial (the second Adam), Hermes, Enoch (Arkhnourh), Idriss, John, Ismaïl b. Muhammad el Tamimi, the missionary.

At the time of Muhammad b. Abdallah, he was called: El -Moqdâd.

Q: Who are the Old and the Eternal?

A: The Elder is Hamza and the Eternal is his brother Ishmael, the Nafs (Soul).

Q: Who are the feet of the Candlestick. (11)

A: These are the three Warnings

Q: Who are these three Warnings?

A: They are John, Mark and Matthew. (12)

Q: How long have they preached?

A: Twenty-one years old.

Each preached 7.

Q: What are these buildings that are in Egypt and are called the Pyramids?

A: These Pyramids were built by the Almighty to achieve a purpose full of wisdom and which he designed in his providence.

Q: What is this wise goal?

A: It is to place and keep there until the day of judgment when will be his second coming the Covenants and Receipts that his divine hand has taken from all creatures. (13)

Q: Why did he appear with each new Law?

A: To exalt his true believers so that they may strengthen themselves there and know that it is he who changes the Justices according to his will and that they no longer believe in anyone but him.

Q: How do souls return to their bodies?

A: Every time a man dies another is born and that is how the world is. (14)

Q: What are Muslims called?

A: El Tanzil (the descent)

Q: What are Christians called?

A: El Ta'wil (Explanation).

These two names (El Tanzil and El Ta'wil) mean for Christians that they have explained the word of the Gospel and for Muslims the widespread rumor that the Quran has come down from Heaven.

Q: For what purpose did God create the Genii (Djinns) and Angels referred to in Hamza's Book of Wisdom?

A: Djinns, Spirits and Demons are like men who did not obey the invitation of our Lord Hakim.

Demons are Spirits before those who have bodies.

As for the Angels, they are a representation of the true worshipers of God, of those who obeyed the invitation of Hakim, who is the Lord worshiped in all the revolutions of the ages.

Q: What are Age Revolutions (Cycles)?

A: These Cycles are the laws of (false) Prophets, that is, those that people of the outer religion (Sunnah) regard as Prophets such as: Adam, Noah, Abraham, Moses, Issa, Muhammad and Said.

All these are one and the same soul; it has transmigrated from one body to another.

They are all demons (Iblis), the cursed one who is Harat b. Termah, who is

Adam the rebel whom God drove out of Paradise, that is, our Lord removed him from the knowledge of his Unity. (15)

Q: Who are the supreme angels who carry the throne of Our Lord?

A: These are the Five Ministers (Hudud) namely:

Gabriel who is Hamza; Michel who is his second brother; Israphil; Azraïl and Mastaroun. Gabriel is Hamza, Michael is Muhammad b. Wahab, Israphil is Salama b. Abdel Wahhab, Azraïl is Bahaeddine, Mastaroun is Ali b. Ahmad.

It is Five Ministers are also called: The Previous (Sâbiq), the Following (Tali), the Application (Hadd), the Opening (Fateh) and the Phantom (Khayal).

Q: What are the four women?

A: They are called Ismail, Muhammad, Salama and Ali, who are also the Word, the Soul, Bahaeddine and Oum el Kheir (the mother of good).

Q: What is the gospel of Christians and what should we think about it?

A: The Gospel did indeed come out of the mouth of the Lord the Messiah, who was Salman el Farsi in the Cycle of Muhammed which Messiah is Hamza b.Ali in the Cycle of El Hakim.

The false Messiah is the one who was born of Mary because he is the son of Joseph.

Q: Where was the True Messiah when the false Messiah was with his Apostles?

A: He was with him, among his Apostles. He preached the gospel and taught the Messiah the son of Joseph.

He said to him: "Do this and that", according to the prescriptions of the Christian religion. He (Joseph's son) listened to him in everything he said.

But when he disobeyed the True Messiah, he put hatred in the hearts of the Jews who crucified him.

Q: What happened after he was crucified?

A: He was put in a tomb.

The True Messiah arrived, stole the body from the tomb and buried it in the garden, then spread the rumor that the Messiah had risen.

Q: Why was the True Messiah behaving like this?

A: To make the Christian religion last and give it more strength.

Q: And why did he promote heresy?

A: So that the Druze could cover themselves with a veil of the religion of the Messiah and that no one knew them for the Druze.

Q: Who is the one who came out of the tomb and entered the Disciples with the doors closed?

A: The living Messiah, who does not die and who is Hamza.

Q: Who revealed the gospel and preached it?

A: Matthieu, Marc, Luc and Jean. These are the four women we talked about.

Q: How is it that Christians did not enter the Unitarian religion?

A: In order to show the action of God who is El Hakim: he does what he wants and as he wants.

Q: How does God accept evil and unbelief?

A: It is our Lord's habit to lead some astray and enlighten others, as it says in the Quran:

"He recognized some and turned away from others" (16)

Q: Why did Hamza son of Ali order us to hide wisdom and not reveal it?

A: Because it contains the secrets and the receipt of Our Lord and we must not discover to anyone things where the salvation of souls and the life of spirits are locked up.

Q: So we are selfish since we don't want everyone to be saved?

A: There is no egoism there because the invitation is withdrawn, the door is closed, is a heretic who is a heretic and a believer who is a believer and everything is as it should be. Lent, which was once ordained, is abolished today, but when a man does Lent outside of the prescribed time and mortifies himself by fasting, this is commendable, because it brings us closer to the divinity.

Q: Why was almsgiving eliminated?

A: With us, alms to our brothers the Druze is just; but it is a crime against all others and it must not be done.

Q: What is the goal of the lonely mortifying himself?

A: That of deserving, when Hakim comes, which he gives to each according to his works, vizirates, pachaliks and governments. (17)

Explanations and Comments:

(1) The Druze in this Catechism is above all "al Talib" (The Student), in the sacred sense of the term. He is reminded of certain fundamental traditions and essential rules. The literal meaning (Apparent = Exoteric or Zaher) is sometimes true, but often it also symbolizes the way to initiation and to "Batin" = Hidden (to the Esoteric).

As for example to the question:

What is the day of judgment?

The answer is:

It is the one where the Creator will appear with a human figure and where he will rule the universe by power and the sword.

This day of judgment relates to the opening of the last portals. Under the human appearance, it is then the divine will which manifests itself and it does so "by the power and the sword, the sword which here symbolizes the end of the existence of illusion, the" entrenchment of profane life. ".

(2) The Renegades are Muslims who left Druzism to return to Islam because they had falsely embraced Druzism and the true worshipers of God (the Unitarians).

(3) The last five names are those of the five Fatimid caliphs. And the three Aliya, El-Mou'il and Abu Zakaria, these are the three Imams hidden in Ismailism. As for El -Aliy, it is the first manifestation of God on earth. Between him and El Bâr, 343 million years ago.

Indeed for Hamza the history of Druzism does not begin with Adam.
Between the establishment of the Universal Intellect and the appearance of Adam, 70 cycles took place, each cycle being composed of 70 weeks and each week of 70 years while a year is the equivalent of 1000 years, i.e. one year. total of 343 million years!

Kamal Joumblatt said:

"Westerners count by a thousand years, we by millions and tens of millions of years."

(4) A few million years ago; "Imaginary city?").

(5) These are the different reincarnations of Hamza:

- Chattnil is the name of Hamza in Adam's time.

- Saïd is Obaïdallah el Mahdi, the founder of the Fatimids.

- Saleh is a prophet of Islam.

The "Hudud" of the different eras following the writings of Hamza and Tamimi can be summarized as follows:

From the Human cycle:

- Our Lord appeared in the form of Al Bâr.

- The Intellect will be in the form of the first Adam "the pure and universal Adam" called Chattnil.
Originally from India, Chattnil emigrated to Yemen, where he organized his Da'wa in favor of the Tawhid of Al Bâr.

- The Soul took on the appearance of the second Adam "the rebellious and partial Adam" the Adam of the Bible and the Koran, known as Enoch

(Ahnûh).

- The Word was manifested in the third Adam "the forgetting and material Adam" who is none other than Eve named Seth.

- the Adversary took on the appearance of Iblis, then called Harit b. Tarmah.

(6) The religion of "Zaher" (Exoteric) or "revelation" is Sunnism; while the religion of "Batin" (Esoteric) or "interpretation" is Shiism.
As for Druzism, it is the "third way" or "Unitarian Religion".

(7) "Knowledge" is among the Druze, an essential condition of religion. Hence the nickname they give themselves "Bani Maarouf", that is to say "Those who know the divinity in humanity".

(8) According to the Druze Dictionary "Luminous Pearls", Myrobolan is a "strong medicine"; it symbolizes the Epistles in which are found the Truths of Druzism, the Presumptions, the names of the Ministers and the Maqâmat.

(9) As a reminder: The five ministers are respectively: Universal Intelligence (the Akl); the Universal Soul (the Nafs); the Previous or the Right Wing (the Sâbiq) and the Following or the Left Wing (the Tâli).
(10) Doumassa or "Zou-Massa" is Ismaïl "the man with the lollipop" because he sucked on the science of Hamza.

(11) The "Candlestick" on which we place the candle of the Unitary Religion.

(12) These Evangelists represent, in Druzism, the Nafs (Ishmael), the Kalima

(Muhammad) and the Sâbiq (Abou El Kheir).

 As for Luke, he represents Bahaedinne.

The True Messiah who is Eleazar is Hamza.

(13) Each Druze who receives "religion" must write the Pact with his own hand and undertake to observe it (see initiation among the Druze below).

This written Pact is kept in Cairo in the Pyramids until the Day of Resurrection.

(14) Souls, according to the Druze belief, do not increase or decrease in number.

(15) There was at the beginning, as we saw in (4), "Universal Intelligence" and its "Adversary".

This Adversary was called, in the Cycle of El Aliy, Hareth b. Termah.

In the Cycle of El Bâr, it was Iblis or Adam the rebel, because he revolted against the "Aql", the First Adam; and because of his rebellion he was cast out of Paradise.

Paradise is the Call to unity religion.

(16) Quran LXVI, 3

(17) By referring to the "Pachaliks" this confirms that the "Catechism of the Druzes" was written in the 16th century, ie five centuries after the birth of Druzism.

Chapter III

The announcement of the advent of their Messiah at the beginning of the 21st century

We have seen that Caliph Al Hakim Bi-Amrallah was born on August 13, 985 and his occultation took place on February 13, 1021.

At the time he was born, all the planets were united in the sign of Cancer, and Saturn presided over the hour in which he was born.

Hakim is cosmically called Albar.

The latter was embodied, as we have just seen, ten times in various parts of the world, in particular in India, in Persia.

Now the Order of the Druze has cycles of progression and relative decline, and this is expressed by its belief in the appearance, at each age of a Messiah, of a Divine envoy.

They have a particular predilection for dividing the history of the world into cycles formed from 7 millennial periods.

These periods of a thousand years, more exactly 960 solar years since it is a thousand lunar years, are announced by the successive appearances of the 7 great prophets and are subject to the successive influences of the 7 planets.

These predictions are based on the return in conjunction of Saturn and Jupiter, respectively every 960 years.

The times when these appearances take place are called Revolutions among the Druze.

They take place "to put the lost on the right path".

The "revolutions", the "periods" where these "revelations" take place, this struggle, on the symbolic level, "of Good against Evil", or "of the Sons of Light against the Sons of Darkness" take place every year. a thousand years.

So the next incarnation of Hakim will take place like the previous ones, at a time when all the planets known to the ancients will come together in a certain zodiacal sign.

By adding to the date of the occultation of Hakim which is in February 1021, 960 solar years which correspond to the Thousand lunar years we obtain: 1021 + 960 = 1981.

The new Mahdi expected by the Druze would therefore be born in February 1981!

Knowing that for the Druze it is often around their forties that a Druze chooses his spiritual path.

We must therefore expect that it begins to manifest itself during the year 2021 (1981 + 40) which would correspond to a Thousand years after Caliph Hakim entered into occultation in 1021!

This coming of the Messiah corresponds to the passage from the Age of Pisces to the Age of Aquarius.

We have had the era of Taurus that tradition equates to the influence of

Babylonian civilization, then the era of Aries with which we traditionally associate the development of Egyptian, Greek and Roman civilizations, then the era of Pisces which is assimilated to Year 0 which corresponds to the birth of Christ (the first Christians had for symbol a Pisces and not the Cross).

The Age of Aquarius, according to esotericists, would mark the advent of Knowledge and Wisdom on Earth.

Note in passing that according to a famous American clairvoyant Madame Dixon, the Mehdi was born on February 5, 1962.

She predicted the following:

"A child born somewhere in the Middle East shortly after seven in the morning on February 5, 1962 will revolutionize the world.

Mankind will begin to feel the power of this man around the beginning of the year 1980 and over the next ten years ".

It is clear that after almost sixty years no "Mahdi" has appeared. This forecast therefore turns out to be false.

Would Bahaeddine be the new Mahdi long awaited by the Druze ? : Another reading of the Druze Origin and Doctrine!

The author of "The Secret Doctrine" the esotericist Helena Blavatsky (1831-1891), founder of the Theosophical movement, during one of her trips to the East visited Lebanon in early 1865, where she was initiated into the Druze religion.

Here is what she wrote at the time regarding her allegations of her membership in Buddhism:

"People call me and think I am a 'follower' (of Buddhism). They believe I was initiated into the pagodas!

[….] I know India and its customs too well … that no European man, let alone a woman, could ever enter the inner recesses of the pagodas.

But I have had many friends among the Buddhists and I have known two Brahmins well and learned a lot from their doctrine.

I belong to the secret sect of the Druze of Mount Lebanon and have spent a long life among dervishes, Persian mullahs and mystics of all kinds. "

From her many travels Madame Blavatsky had known followers of many races, from northern and southern India, Tibet, Persia, China, Egypt and various European, Greek, Hungarian, Italian nations. , English as well as certain breeds in South America.

Now Helena Blavatsky refutes and questions the knowledge received about the origin and religion of the Druze.

Indeed in an article published in the theosophical review titled "Lamas and Druzes" (June-July 1983), she argues that Al-Hakim was not the founder of the Druze religion.

For her, the Druze are the descendants of the persecuted mystics of all nations who took refuge in the mountains of Lebanon during the early years of the Christian era.

The Gnostic strain in their religious philosophy came to them from the Gnostic Ophites who fled to Syria and Lebanon during the second century in order to escape the persecution of the Christian Church.

Some Druze trace their Order back to Hamza, Muhammad's uncle who in 625 went to Tibet in search of secret wisdom.

He is said to have been reincarnated in the eleventh century as Hamza, the Caliph and founder of the Druze, in the same way that the Buddha reincarnated in the Tibetan Lamas and Nanak in the Guru-Kings of the Sikhs.

The Druze, according to Madame Blavatsky, are in fact the Sikhs of Asia Minor, the similarity between them being the result of their mutual connection with a third community, even more mysterious, that of the Brotherhood of Tibetan Lamaists known as the "Brotherhood of Khe-Lang".

(Note that the Khe-lang brotherhood refers to the community (saṅgha) of Tibetan Buddhist monks).

Madame Blavatsky considers that the unity of everything in the universe implies and justifies our belief in the existence of knowledge that is at the same time scientific, philosophical and religious, proving the necessity and the reality of a link between man and everything that exists in the universe; this knowledge becomes essentially RELIGION, and, considered in its integrity and universality; it is called "RELIGION-WISDOM" and that the

Druze are the last survivors of this religion, which is a practical mystic and whose branches are Kabalism, Theosophy and Occultism.

In the cited article, Blavastsky writes that just as the Tibetan BODHISATTVAS are embodiments of the spirit of Buddha, the Okals (Sages) Druze are the embodiments of Hamza.

The two peoples have a real system of words, passwords and recognition signals between neophytes, and we know that they are almost identical, for they are, in part, those of the Theosophists.

In the Druze mystical system, there are five "messengers" or interpreters of the "Word of Supreme Wisdom" which are equivalent to the five main BODHISATTVAS of Tibet, each of which is the bodily temple of the spirit of one of the five Buddhas.

The titles of the five main Druze "messengers"are:

1- **Hamza** (Spiritual Wisdom), considered as the Messiah through whom the incarnate Wisdom speaks.

2- **Ismail Al Tamimi** (the Universal Soul).

He prepares the Druze before their initiation to receive "Wisdom".

3- Abu Abdallah Mohamed Ibn Wahab **Al Qorachi** (the Word).

His duty is to watch the conduct and the needs of the brothers: a kind of

Bishop.

4- **Abulkhair as-Samini** (the one above) called "the Right Wing".

5- **Bahaedinne Al Moqtana** (the "Next") called the "Left Wing".

These last two Samini and Bahaeddine are both messengers between Hamza and the brotherhood.

Above these living mediators who remain forever unknown to all, except the "Okals" (Sages), stand the ten Incarnations of the "Supreme Wisdom", the last of which is due to return at the end of the cycle, which is fast approaching. not (expected in the 21st century, although no one outside Hamza knows the day), this last "messenger" in accordance with the cyclical recurrence of events being also the first that came with Hamza, hence Bahaeddin.

There are also five living or incarnated Buddhas, the main one being the Dalai Lama, called "Ocean of Wisdom".

Above him, as above Hamza, there is the "Supreme Wisdom": the abstract principle from which emanated the Five Buddhas, the Master Buddha (the last Bodhisattva, or Vishnu in the avatar Kalki, the last avatar of God Vishnu, in Hinduism -), the tenth "messenger" expected on earth.

But it will be the One Wisdom and it will be embodied in the whole of humanity taken collectively and not individually.

The Five BODHISATTVAS are in order:

1- The **Dalai Lama**, the embodiment of "spiritual" wisdom that comes from Siddhartha Gautama.

2- **Bande-cha-an Rem-boo-tchi**. He is "the" active "earthly wisdom.

3- **Sa-Dcha-Fo**, or the "Buddha's Spokesman".

4- **Khi-sson-Tamba**, the "Precursor" (of Buddha) to the Grand Kooren.

5- **Tchang-Zya-Fo-Lang**, in the Altai mountains. He is called the "Successor" (of Buddha).

The "Shaberons" (term related to Tibetan zhabs) are less than one degree of BODHISATTVAS.

They are like the chief Okals of the Druze, the "initiates" of the great wisdom or the esoteric religion of Siddhartha Gautama.

This double list of the "Five" shows a great resemblance between the Lamas and Druze.

This is also manifested by their mystical statistics.
Indeed, they estimate the entire human race at 1,332 million.

They say that when good and evil come to equilibrium in the scale of human actions (now evil is by far the heaviest), then the breath of "Wisdom" will wipe out 666 million in the blink of an eye. men exactly.

The 666 million survivors will have the "Supreme Wisdom" embodied in them.

This probably has an allegorical meaning and may have a relation to the number of the "great beast" of the Apocalypse of Saint John!

The Druze claim that Hamza today is hidden in a secret retreat known only to his Initiates.

Every seventh year, some of these Initiates go to a certain place in the western part of China, returning at the end of the eleventh year with new instructions from Hamza.

And Madame Blavatsky concludes:

"As Samini and Behaeddine are the sole custodians of the secret of Hamza's retreat, and having the means to consult their Master, from time to time they make known his directives and commandments to the Brotherhood, and thus, even now the two Okals who bear these names set out every 7 years, through Basra and Persia to Tartary and Tibet and to the western end of China and return at the expiration of the eleventh year, bringing new orders of Hamza.

"As a result of the expected war between China and Russia, just last year a Druze messenger passed through Bombay on his way to Tibet and Tartary.

This would explain "the superstitious belief" that "the souls of all pious Druze are supposed to occupy certain cities in China in large numbers."

It is around the plateau of Pamirs - it is said in agreement with scholars specialists of the Bible, that the cradle of the true race must be situated; but the cradle of the only initiated humanity, of those who have tasted for the first time the fruit of knowledge, and these are to be found in Tibet, Mongolia, Tartary, China and India: there too, souls pious and initiated brothers transmigrate and become "Sons of God".

Every theosophist should know what this language means.

They challenge the fable of Adam and Eve and say that those who first ate the forbidden fruit and thus became "Elohim" were Enoch or Hermes (the supposed father of Freemasonry) and Seth or Sat-an father of wisdom and secret knowledge, whose residence, they say, is now on the planet Mercury (the Buddha means Wise and Mercury is the God of Wisdom according to Hermes and the planet consecrated to Siddhartha Gautama is Mercury) and that the Christians have been kind enough to convert into a chief demon, "the fallen angel."

Their devil is an abstract principle and is called the "Rival".

"Millions of Chinese Unitarians" can mean Tibetan Lamas, Hindus and other Orientals, as well as the Chinese.

It is true that the Druze believe in their day of resurrection and await it in the final battle of Armageddon, which he pronounces "Ramdagon".

Since the word Armageddon is found in Revelation, one would think that the Druze found the idea in the Revelation of Saint John! It is not so.

On this day which, according to the teaching of the Druze, "will see the consummation of the great spiritual plane", the bodies of the sages and devotees will be absorbed in absolute essence, and undergoing transformation will pass from the many to the "ONE".

This is the Buddhist idea of Nirvana.

Their "Persian Magic and Gnosticism" make them regard Saint John as Oannes, the Chaldean fish-man, and suddenly connects their belief at the same time with the Indian Vishnu and the Lamaic symbolism.

Their "Armageddon" is simply "Ramdagon", the word Ramdagon possibly being the anagram of Armageddon, meaning "Rama-Dagon" ("Rama" of the solar race is an incarnation of Vishnu, a Sun-God, and "Dagon" or the Chaldean Holy Wisdom incarnated in their "Messenger", Oannes - the Fish-Man, and descending on the "Sons of God" that is to say the Initiates of any country and so it is that everything is explained".

Chapter IV

The Key to the Druze Mysteries:
The symbolism of their colors in the light
of the high Masonic ranks

In the Quran at Sura 16 (The Bees), we can read in Verse 13:

"In that He (Allah) has scattered over the earth, in different colors, in this, verily, is surely a sign for a people who are building themselves up."

Thus, the colors that shine on the earth correspond to the nuances that the seer perceives in the spirit world where everything is spiritual and therefore significant.

This symbolism and mysticism of colors is very present in Druze society.

The One Hundred and Eleven Letters of Wisdom are often written in color.

The Five red dots characterize the Five Great Ministers of the unitary hierarchy.

The five black dots above certain words designate bad ministers of false religions (the "blameworthy" Hududs).

The five red dots placed horizontally on a word or a name refer to "laudable" Hudud.

These Five Great Ministers are each associated with a color:

Hamza (Intelligence) is associated with **Green**
Tamîmî (Soul) is associated with **Red**
Qurachî (the Word) is associated with **Yellow**

Samurrî (the Previous) is associated with **Blue**

Bahâ el Din (the Next) is associated with the **White**

The Five colors which respectively symbolize the hypostases of the Pentad are found in the Druze flag (a green triangle on the left edge and four stripes, red, yellow, blue and white), or in the fabrics which surround the catafalques of the Saints in their tombs establishing a formal hierarchy between them.

This is an arcane principle that makes it possible to recognize each of the figures of the Pentad, if it were to appear: the color of the clothes would allow them to be identified and their rank in the hierarchy to be known.

The colors therefore reflect what the body reflects in light regardless of the perspective in which one is located.

Whether it is body, soul or spirit, colors are always meant to reflect the energy contained.

If we start from black, we consider that we must see in this color the energy translated into activatable matter.
In other words, this material corresponds both to what is the poorest in light, but also to what is fairly easy to handle.

This is consistent with the idea that the Negro translates both matter in its most primitive form and the action that can be exerted on it in the material world.

Red expresses energy in itself, as if the energy were an object independent of the person expressing it.

On the other hand, if this energy is considered to be seen by humans, it will be symbolically translated as yellow like the Sun, which symbolizes the energy that matters to terrestrial man.

Blue and **White** are two colors that have to do with the mind, that is, with what is sometimes called the most intangible light or the most primordial and elusive energy.

From this perspective, it is easy to evoke **White**, who is said, in a banal way, to be the sum of all the colors: the color white unites all the Unitarians to Bahâ el Din.

On the other hand, **Blue** expresses depth, which is to say that it is about the Spirit seen from within man.

How not to evoke it through meditation?

Man turns to himself to recognize the Spirit which he carries and who can truly enlighten him.

Spiritual energy, inner dynamism and serene peace can then easily coexist through an alchemy that marks the richness of life.

It remains now to consider the last color, the one associated with Imam Hamza and which will play a major role: **Green**

It could not be better defined than by relating to it what the alchemists called mercury water.

It is that **Green** translates what is transitory, such as changes of shape, and it ensures the link between them.

Without it, we cannot translate the dynamics of an organization.

In Freemasonry, we find the symbolism of colors in all the rites especially in the thirty three degrees of the Old and Accepted Scottish Rite.

This is how in the third degree that of Master, the apron is white and edged in red (In the Grand Orient at the French Rite the apron is white with a blue edging).

The cord is blue and edged in red.

Compared to the first two degrees (Apprentice and Companion) where one moved in an energetic and spiritual environment (white apron) without symbolically having much hold over other than by acting, a differentiation takes place at the third.

The Master Mason begins to internalize all of this.

He begins to spiritualize and apprehend the spirit from within as indicated by the reference to blue.

Thus, to build his environment, the Master Mason makes the spirit (Blue) cohabit on his cord with the externalized energy (Red) and the externalized spirit (White).

Green appears for the first time with the fifth degree: the Perfect Master.

It indicates an interface area.

Green is therefore the triumph of the ternary in all that is achieved.

This is the call to order.

The different colors of the Druze symbolism we find them in Freemasonry at the thirtieth degree: the Knight Kaddosch.

This degree is the one with which the Masonic initiation ends.

In his "Voyage en Orient", Gérard de Nerval, compared the Sheikh Aql Druze to the Chevalier Kaddosch.

As for the lodge of the thirtieth degree, it is decorated with five colors:

White, Blue, Red and Yellow appear in the Three Candles.

Behind the throne are the standards of the Order with two crossed Green bands.

Indeed, the color Green holds an important place among the Druze as well as among the Freemasons.

Among the Druze, it is associated with Intelligence embodied by the founder of Druzism Hamza Ibn Ali called the "Master of Time" (Qâ'im al Zaman).

Among the Freemasons, the presence of Green in some degrees and not in others, suggests that the Scottish initiation constitutes a man's march towards more truth.

In other words, these degrees would unfold in an ascending spiral and each passage through **Green** would then correspond to access to a new spiral (These spirals would correspond to the Ten cycles of the Druze).

Green is the color of emerald.

To better understand its importance, it is good to refer to the text of the Emerald Table, well known to the disciples of Hermes Trismegistus such as the Freemasons and the Unitarians (Druze):

"It is true, without lie, certain and true, What is below as what is above, and what is above as what is below; by these things are and come from One, by the mediation of One, so all things are born of this one thing by adaptation."

"The Sun is the father, and the Moon the mother. The Wind carried him in his belly. The Earth is its nurse and its receptacle.

The Father of all Thelema (primitive substance from which everything was formed and which according to Hermes Trismegistus is both Heaven and Earth: subtle and fixed) of the universal world is here.

Its strength or power remains intact, if it is converted into Earth.

You will separate the Earth from the fire, the subtle from the thick, gently, with great industry.

He ascends from Earth and descends from Heaven, and receives strength from higher things and lower things.

By this means you will have the glory of the world, strong in all strength, for it will overcome all subtle things and penetrate all solid things.

So the world was created.

From that will emerge admirable adaptations, of which the means are given here ".

"This is why I was called Hermes Trismegistus, having the three parts of universal philosophy."

"What I have said about the solar work is complete."

Inspired by the Emerald Table, an anonymous treatise "Mukhtassar al Bayân" develops Druze cosmology:

"Matter (Hyle) constitutes the source of all that is sensitive.
It comes from five ministers and therefore is inherently good.

By its movement, it forms the four elements (fire, air, water, earth), the four qualities (heat, cold, humidity, drought), the twelve signs of the Zodiac and the seven planets, each of which inhabits a sphere, namely: Saturn, Jupiter, Mars, Sun, Venus, Mercury and the Moon.

In each element, there are two properties: density and subtlety.

The elements, the spheres and the stars, by combining their action on the earth, generate the three kingdoms of nature: the mineral kingdom, the vegetable kingdom and the animal kingdom, to which human bodies belong, created by speaking souls ".

Moreover, as we saw in Chapter III, the Tibetan BODHISATTVAS are incarnations of the spirit of Buddha, the Okals (Sages) Druze are the incarnations of Hamza and that in the mystical system of the Druze there are five "messengers" or interpreters of the "Word of Supreme Wisdom" which are equivalent to the five main BODHISATTVAS of Tibet, each of which is the bodily temple of the spirit of one of the five Buddhas.

As among the Druze, the main colors of Buddhism are thus traditionally 5 in number, like the 5 wisdom Buddhas: Green, Red, Yellow, Blue and White.

One of the significant uses of color in Buddhism stems from a concept called "rainbow body", "light body", or Jalu in Tibetan.

This concept covers the highest state that the meditator's mind can access before leaving Samsara, repetition of suffering and dissatisfaction, cycle of rebirths.

It is a state of transition where the meditator's body sublimates and merges into pure light to finally reach the state of Nirvana, that is to say of awakening and liberation from the cycle of reincarnations, the colors converging in one only intense white light.

Thus, the idea of a rainbow body like the projection of a prism contains within it all the possible manifestations of light and therefore of color.

The light body is inner awakening.

Understanding the principles suggested by these colors, applying this wisdom to life and releasing desires is how the rainbow body, and potentially nirvana, is achieved.

So:

Green corresponds to: **Hamza** (Spiritual Wisdom), considered to be the Messiah through whom incarnate Wisdom speaks and to the **Dalai Lama**, the embodiment of "spiritual" wisdom which comes from Siddhartha Gautama.

Red corresponds to **Ismail Al Tamimi** (the Universal Soul) and **Bande-cha-an Rem-boo-tchi**. He is "the" active "earthly wisdom.

The **Yellow** corresponds to Abu Abdallah Mohamed Ibn Wahab **Al Qorachi** (the Word) and to **Sa-Dcha-Fo**, or the "Buddha's Spokesman".

Blue corresponds to Abulkhair **as-Samini** (the one above) called "the Right Wing" and to **Khi-sson-Tamba**, the "Forerunner" (of Buddha) to the Great Kooren.

Finally to **White** corresponds to **Bahaedinne Al Moqtana** (the "Next") called "Left Wing" and to **Tchang-Zya-Fo-Lang**, in the Altai mountains.

He is called the "Successor" (of Buddha).

Chapter V
Other points of convergence
with Freemasonry

a - Children of the Light: From Tawhid to the Great Architect of the Universe (GADLU)

b - The different Degrees of Initiation (initiation, ritual, symbol, numerology, gematria and kabbalistic analysis ...)

c - The Druze filiation of the Rite of Memphis-Misraïm

d - Hudud and Landmark

e - John the Evangelist

f - Concept of freedom, equality and fraternity

The Druze would they be the upholders of the long initiatory chain which, since the beginning of time, transmitted the knowledge that Plato claimed can only be given to those who are prepared for it?

For Gérard de Nerval, the religion of the Druze is only a syncretism of all the religions and all the previous philosophies.

And for Kamal Joumblatt, this was beyond doubt.

He defined the Druze as follows:

"The Druze is not just the name of those we call 'Druze', this sect that is found in Lebanon or Syria, Israel, or Turkey and even northern Pakistan.

Is Druze any monotheist, believing in the unity of the religions of the world with their rites and doctrines.

It is a name that applies to Christians, Buddhists, Muslims and Hindus. "

and add:

"We are a people of 5,000 years old and we hold certain sacred works of Ancient Egypt, notably the secret work of Hermes Trismegistus, known in our country as Imhotep.

It was he who built the first pyramid at Sakkarah, one of the first initiatory centers of antiquity.

Pythagoras went there, was initiated there, and created the Order of the Pythagoreans.

One of the most mysterious links in this chain was the priest-king Melchisedec, initiator of Abraham.

One of the most important was Jethro, initiator of Moses; he is particularly revered among us.

As for Christ, its initiator was John the Baptist.

The Druze are currently one of the links in this great chain which can also be the true Universal Brotherhood.

Thus at Sakkarah on the banks of the Nile, in Babylon on the banks of the Euphrates, at Qumran on the Dead Sea, among the Templars in Jerusalem, the initiation was but one, as it is today in the Himalayas, in the Highlands of Scotland, in the Andes and in Mount Lebanon.

They are all followers of the Unity, but divided under other names in other religions.

Indeed, in the Druze books available, there appear various sources of inspiration from the ancient world first.

The Egypt of the Pyramid of Saqqara recalls the role of Imhotep, architect and physician assimilated to Hermes Trismegistus.

From the Old Testament, Melchisedec is celebrated as the initiator of Abraham; Jethro priest of Midian is known as Chouaib, stepfather and initiator of Moses.

From Greek philosophy, are retained the concepts of the unity of the universe in God, and the return of this fundamental Unity through successive cycles of learning of Knowledge.

In the New Testament, the character of Lazarus is used, along with a number of Manichean borrowings.

In the Qur'an, verses interpreted as revealing conceptions of Initiation and Reincarnation are emphasized.

For millennia, these doctrines have come through different means of expression and languages.

Despite sometimes erroneous interpretations, they all come together to serve as a Principle of Moral Law for a Human Fraternity.

This theory resembles the Masonic instruction of the second degree, that of Fellow Craft, where we find one of the symbolic journeys consisting in studying and comparing the great philosophical, moral and religious doctrines which were transmitted through the centuries by great initiates. such as Hermes Trismegistus, Pythagoras, Moses, Plato, Abraham, Jesus, Confucius ..

The study of the secret teachings confirms that the Druze community is above all comparable to that of the Essenes, the Templars, the original Rosicrucians and the Pythagoreans, whose roots come from Egypt.

Like the Essenes, the Druze are made up of an outer circle, the Druze people, and a circle of initiates, the Okals, which means "Sages".

These Okals, considered to be holders of inviolable secrets, would be in constant contact with the hidden rulers of our planet, who are perfect beings known in the West as the Great White Brotherhood.

This relationship has already been mentioned by one of them, known as KH (Koot Houmi, a master of wisdom from Kashmir, India) in "The Letters of Mahatmas", from which the following paragraph is taken:

"What they keep is that two of our supporters have met the Druze brothers and that three others are already on the way".

For esotericists, there is a tradition called the Primordial Tradition, a legacy of scientific, philosophical and mystical knowledge, a secret

gnosis which deals with the hidden laws of nature and the true position of man in the universe.

This knowledge is accompanied in those who hold it with a certain power.

It was the prerogative of civilizations prior to those we know, it has nevertheless been transmitted to our present humanity through the channel of the schools of Mysteries and Initiation.

This initiatory light, ancient Egypt would have possessed.

This is why the initiation schools of the East and the West trace their origins back to this civilization.

This is particularly the case with the Druze, the Rose-Croix and Freemasonry.

Indeed, the Great White Brotherhood was founded in its primitive form by Pharaoh Thoutmose III (1447 BC) who established the important laws of the Brotherhood.

In 1378 BC the great-grandson of Thutmose III, Pharaoh Amenophis IV - known as "Akhenaton" became the great reformer of the secret organization.

In the "Schools of Life" founded under Thoutmose III and Akhenaton, the pupils were severely selected, gathered around the Pharaoh, they studied the knowledge of their Atlantean Initiators in a form adapted for them.

It was therefore in 1350 BC that what would later be called the Great White Brotherhood was born, to which the sect of the Therapists in Greece and the Essenes in Palestine was attached.

The Tradition then spread from Egypt to China and India where Kamal Joumblatt was initiated.

a- The Children of the Light: From Tawheed to the Great Architect of the Universe

In the Beginning, there was the Word, synonymous with Divine Action.

The Great Architect of the Universe, wanted to magnify his Love, and Create "from here below", by endowing his Creature with Spirit, Divine Immaterial Substance, to access Universal Consciousness.

This "Primordial Light Energy" caused the Emanation of Spirit.

Thus, the Being is both "Divine Matter" and "Spiritual Energy".

This Emanation, dear to PLOTIN, is the product of the ONE or of the DIVINE Oneness (AL TAWHID), Unique, Indivisible and Indivisible, Universal and Cosmic.

PYTHAGORAS considers the One, Creator, Center and Origin of all things.

Thus the Universe took shape through a series of processional Mysteries, not only in Creative Harmony, but also in a succession of phenomena and relationships incomprehensible to Man.

This Universal Harmonious Balance is a reflection of the well-codified Architecture on the Cosmic Scale.

The Logos is not only Consciousness of this Balanced Architecture, where Numbers and Measures are Immortally and Immutably perpetual, but also a Harmony of Being, through which Druze and Freemasons will make this INITIATIC QUEST, in order to approach their own Consciousness and inevitably to UNIVERSAL CONSCIOUSNESS.

This is how Freemasonry is a GNOSA which, beyond the beliefs of each one, tries to give the Light to those who, through their personal quests, will want to receive it, and to shed light on the homologies in the different beliefs , their crosses and their purposes.

As for the specificity of GNOSE DRUZE (AL OURFAN), it is that it finds its Originality by the representation of the Divine, the Universe and the World.

She was thus able to emphasize the intrinsic Unity of all Abrahamic Monotheisms, but not only, since she integrated Greek Philosophy and Hermeticism in its Egyptian component to build a New Universal and Messianic Vision of the World.

If Druzism and Freemasonry conceive of the One, it is because the One has transmitted to us this piece of LIGHT, since HE IS LIGHT.

These SONS OF LIGHT (Druze and Freemasons) taught and invoked the ONE, in Space and Time, measurable dimensions of Matter and History, Geography and Civilizations.

But the Essence and the Finality of the Universal consciousness are not limited by these data Perceptible by our Senses and our intelligence.

Because One is in Time and out of Time, HE is in an Unlimited Universe that He has Created.

Phenomenologists, Structuralists, even Epicureans and others have perceived only the material face of Existence, while HERMES, PYTHAGORE, PLATO, MANI, MOISE, JESUS, MAHOMET AND AL HAKIM have been invested with the Revelation of the One, Original Causality, Existing outside of all Existence, by Necessity and by His Will (and the Word became Flesh; Gospel of John).

Historical continuity, corollary of this periodic Divine impulse, from THOTH or HERMES, to the Ismaili and Druze Revelations (HAMZA), via the ESSENIANS, to end in the magnificent Illustration of the GREAT ARCHITECT OF THE UNIVERSE in our Masonic Spiritual Elevation and Unitarian (TAWHID); Continuity that has never ceased (Initiatory Chain or Gold Chain).

The Great Architect of the Universe, thus planted the germ of Love in the heart of Man, because he created it in his Image, and gave him the power to rise up to HIM.

By this Existential INITIATION, so Way of Love, WISDOM, and Spirit.

Druze and Freemasons are CHILDREN OF LIGHT, through the Process of Initiation, and awareness of Divine Existence through Spiritual Transcendence.

We leave the Darkness and walk towards the Light.

And with each step, or Elevation, we leave "Nothingness" to approach the Light Center.

We leave a part of ourselves at each step to be reborn and set out again on the New Journey, with more Light and less Darkness (like in a Temple and a Khalwa).

Pythagoras reminds us of this Center as the Center of the Universe or "the Sacred Spiritual Light".

The Harmony of the Universe guides all things, for anything whatever, must be what it is in order to be.

This can only exist as a function of a Principle of Harmony and therefore of the One.
The disappearance of the I, Non-I relation brings about the disappearance of Duality and produces Knowledge of the One.

It is not about "Finding" something, but on the contrary of making disappear what veils the One.

Master ECKART writes: "God and I are ONE in Knowledge, he who knows and what he knows are ONE. "

Duality or Multiplicity, was an ambiguous manifestation, yet there is no ambiguity in anything that Man can see or conceive; but seeing is not coming out of the Cave to receive the Light.

This ORPHIC tendency of Immortality reminds us that "If you come to know yourself as being made of Life and Light, you will return to Life".

This Initiatic Voyage is a Sublimation of the Soul (NAFS), and the true Odyssey in forty-five thousand towards the Glory of the Universal Spirit (and of the Great Architect of the Universe), by JALAL EDDIN EL ROUMI, as the 'Hypostasis of Divine Love.

Journey leading from Human to Ultra-Human, and from the entire Cosmos to Ultimate Convergence, the Omega point, from which GOD reveals himself as "the One and Absolute Future".

b- Initiations, Rituals, Symbols, Numerology, Gematria and Kabbalistic Analysis ...

It is important to remember that it is among the Druze or among the Freemasons or any initiatory order, initiation is One and there is only one

Truth.

The rite of admission among the Druze marks the precise moment when the candidate passes from a state of "JAHEL" "Ignorance" to a stage of revelation.

Not all Druze are ready for initiation.

As it is said in the Druze catechism, "You have to knock", to prove oneself, because the "Door is closed".

The Druze who wishes to enter religion must begin by adopting an appropriate outward appearance, by which he signals the change that has taken place in his life.

On his way to the Khalwa (Lodge), to the meetings held there on Thursday and Sunday evenings, he introduces himself as a "requester of religion", a request which is addressed primarily to the congregation of Sheikhs (Venerable Masters) of his village, but also to God.

The candidate is in fact subjected to a probationary period of several months during which the Sheikhs observe his general behavior and decide if it is worthy to enter religion, which makes the Druze say: "our religion is difficult, because that religion with us is behavior ".

The decision of the Sheikhs takes into account the candidate's past, what is said about him in the village, but also his present situation and activities.

Asking for religious initiation is ultimately for a Druze a crucial moment when he is faced with the judgment of his society.

For this, the Sheikhs organize a Da'wa (Dress) internal to the community.

The candidate must formally enter into a contract before entering a cycle of initiations.

From the outset, a contract made each Druze the custodian of a truth that should not be divulged: he became the secret guarantor of religion (Kitman el Dinn = law of silence).

After this probationary period, the aspirant is admitted to the first degree of the religious hierarchy and becomes a beginner: Mubtadi 'or Mutadaris (Apprentice).
Initiation is reserved for an elite.
It is also often around 40 that a Druze chooses the spiritual path.

The initiation is also open to women; in fact in the Druze catechism we read the question:

"Is it appropriate for women to be initiated into the secrets of the unitary religion? "

The answer is:

Yes, because our Lord imposed the pact on women also; they obeyed and followed Hakim's call as mentioned in the Epistle "The Covenant of

Women" and in "The Epistle to the Daughters".

To enter a Khalwa, the initiate woman must remove her adornments (jewelry); it is separated from the Sheikh by a curtain.

Women initiates take an oath upon their first presentation in a Khalwa.

Among the Freemasons, the candidate having made his request, the lodge deliberates and appoints three investigative brothers, who do not know each other, and entrusts them with meeting the candidate and writing a report in order to identify his personality as different points of view: it is the individual in himself, the moral man, the social man etc.

This investigation can take several months.

Although each investigating brother is free to ask the layman all the questions he deems useful to inform his judgment, he is responsible for questioning the layman in more depth on his duties towards himself, towards his family. towards humanity.

In possession of the written reports, the Venerable Master, during a holding, proceeds to the deliberation on the admission to the candidate's tests, then to a preliminary test, which consists of questioning the applicant; if the latter has had a favorable vote, he is called for another meeting and taken to a "think tank".

There, the candidate must make his "philosophical and moral testament".

Then, blindfolded, he is introduced to the lodge and questioned by the Venerable and the Masters present.

He is escorted out and the lodge votes on his admission or rejection to the first degree initiation to the grade of Apprentice.

Initiation into some Masonic Obediences is open to women.

The Initiation Ceremony

It takes place in the Khalwa which has two entrance gates, one for women and the other for men.

The Interior is made up of three parts separated by a thick curtain that isolates the women (northern part) from the Sheikh (southern part).

Women can thus hear the words of the Sheikh, but do not see what is happening.

A tiler stands at the entrance to the Khalwa, which is always outside the village, and demands from members who belong to the Druze community, the password, specific signs and touches.

Among these passwords, there is the one that is common to all Druze, who, after greeting each other, ask the question:

"Are there peasants in your country who sow the seed of Myrobolan?"

He must answer:

"It is sown in the hearts of believers".

He is asked if he knows the "Ministers"?

If he answers positively, he is considered a brother; otherwise it is not admitted ".

After a period of probation of two years and if he overcomes the first tests, the initiation of the postulant takes place on the feast of the Adha, celebrated in Islam in memory of the sacrifice of Abraham, in the presence of the Sheikh. Aql (Venerable Master).

The new brother or the new sister writes with his hand a pact of commitment called "Pact of the Master of Time" as follows:

"Me…, I have resolved and decided to put my soul, my body, my goods, my knowledge and all that my right hand and my left hand have, under the obedience of my Lord Al Hakim the Most High, Governor governors, the Most Powerful who rules over all beings and all creatures.

I give myself to him and confide in him. I admit absolutely and perfectly before my brothers and my Lord Imam, that I have renounced all other religions and that I do not want anything that is opposed or contrary to its uniqueness.

I will not say that I have a worshiped God in heaven, nor a revered Imam on earth other than my Great Lord Al Hakim, the Mighty in his works, who rules in his own authority; my help and my help; to him I entrust the conduct of my life;

I wrote this document myself, being of sound mind and body, freely and of my own free will, without coercion or violence. "

Then the Sheikh receives him among the small handful of initiates, strongly urging him to remain silent about the knowledge he has just acquired.

He is then presented with a dish of figs to eat and the Sheikh asks him:

"O man! Do you think that you take religion in the figs and become one of the Oneness? "
The candidate answers:

"Yes, I believe it".

Then the Sheikh gives him a part of the Epistles of Wisdom as well as the habit corresponding to his rank.

The meeting ends with a snack consisting of dried fruits, such as figs, raisins, almonds and nuts.

The precept relating to meetings reads as follows:

"It is necessary, initiates and initiates, that you assemble each Thursday evening, that you read and keep the books of science which Our glorious Lord has left you; you must also teach your initiate sisters behind a curtain, and that they do not raise their voices.

Read the secret vespers among yourselves, because I destroyed the Seven Onerous Precepts and replaced them with Seven Spirituals ".

Women who attend readings should refrain from laughing and crying, because they might arouse the passions of men by these means.

The Seven Druze Precepts recalling the pillars of Islam are:

1 - The Veracity of the language which replaces Prayer

2 - The practice of the Fraternity which replaces the tithe

3 - The abandonment of the cult of nothingness which replaces the Fast

4 - The renunciation of demons which replaces the Pilgrimage

5 - The Confession of Unity which replaces the two Professions of Faith

6 - The contentment of the works of the Lord which replaces the Holy War

7 - Resignation to the Lord's orders which replaces Submission to legitimate authority.

Among Freemasons, the initiation ceremony takes place in the Temple

(Lodge) composed of three parts:

On the side of the North column sit the Apprentices, on the side of the South column sit the Companions and the Venerable Master is in the middle room.

A brother stands at the entrance to the Temple to ensure the regularity of the Brothers by "Tuiling" them on the password, signs and touching.

The candidate's initiation consists of a series of tests or trips.

Once the journeys are over, the layman takes an oath at the Altar of Oaths where the

Three Great Lights of Freemasonry are located and where he contracts the obligation to maintain secrecy by proclaiming:

"I…, under the invocation of the Great Architect of the Universe and in the presence of this Respectable Lodge of Freemasons regularly gathered and duly consecrated, of my own and free will, I solemnly swear on the Three Great Lights of the Free - masonry never to reveal any of the secrets of Freemasonry to those who do not have the capacity to know them, or to trace them, write them, chisel, engrave or sculpt, or reproduce them otherwise ".

The initiation session ends with a meal (Agape) in honor of the new candidate.

It has been seen among the Druze that the act sealing the entry into religion for the aspirant was an oath taken on the book containing the writings of the Druze religion.

The Aspirant now becomes Mubtad'i (Apprentice).

Religious who have reached the end of the learning cycle and possess all of the writings are referred to as Khâtim.

These different degrees appear in the costume.

All Khâtim wear a distinctive clothing mark:

The striped "abaya", whose vertical bands are black, green, red, blue, yellow or white depending on the degree symbolically reached in religion.

For women, their degree of initiation is recognized by the way they tie their veil.

Only the leaders of the religious congregations of each Druze community wear the "laffa medawara" which is the mark of the greatest religious.

Druze initiates are in possession of very old manuscripts.

Some would have reached them by strange, even unusual ways.

Others have yet to be passed on to them.

Once the initiation is completed the new Sheikh Druze should wear black clothes, shave his hair, grow his mustache and wear the laffé.

Depending on his age and knowledge, the attributes of the Sheikh change.

From the age of forty, the "mashayekhs" have distinctive signs marking an explicit hierarchy.

The red jacket is available to all mashayekhs over the age of forty who wish, the red symbolizing freedom or the soul.

It is the universal symbol of fire, divine love and that of sacrifice.

The white and striped jacket is important: it marks a high degree of initiation.

White symbolizes light, purity or the past.

It is obtained by cooptation.

Likewise the highest symbol of the Druze spiritual authorities, the "laffé medawara" is transmitted by the one who wears it to another Sheikh.

There are five hierarchical levels according to a Pyramidal Order:

- The first that of the "mashayekhs" in general

- The second is made up of the "Sais" (Venerable) director of Khalwa

- The third is that of the "mashayekhs" with the white and striped jacket

- The fourth and the fifth degree are those of the "mashayekhs" in the "laffé medawara"

- The highest spiritual authority belongs to the oldest who, in general, has appointed, by co-option, the others.

To initiates, they are offered an esoteric reading of the seven Shiite pillars of the Druze, in relation to the five Sunnis.

Indeed, taking up the Muslim classification of the five obligations of Islam, to which are added two obligatory articles of faith, the act of faith (Chahâdat), prayer (Salat), alms (Zakat), fasting (Saoum), the pilgrimage (Hajj), and the fight of faith (Jihad), as well as the allegiance, for the Shiites, to the Imam (Wilaya), the Druze give a different interpretation, hidden elsewhere, and undoubtedly revealed gradually according to the degree of knowledge of the initiate.

1- The CHAHADA for every Muslim (it suffices to repeat this sentence 3 times in a row, no doubt with conviction, to become it): "There is no god but God, and Mohammad is his Prophet" is analyzed from the following way:

The Oneness of God is the supreme truth, and if Mohammad reinforced its belief, in a ritualistic way, in Islam, the Fatimids and the Imams gave the initiatory key of this Union to be achieved with God in the form of true Faith (IMAN).

2- SALAT (prayer), which must be repeated every day 5 times among pious Muslims, must be constant in the spirit of the Druze; it is a continual incitement to follow the Guide (Al-DÂL), the book (AL-DÂLIL), and the hidden meaning (AL-MADLOUL).

3- Legal alms or ZAKAT, which is calculated on the basis of 10% of the income of any Muslim, must be interpreted, among the Druze, on a moral level; egoism being negative, we must help our fellows, by our example, by our Gnostic knowledge, but also by not putting our contemporaries in a situation of crisis, hence the need to keep the secret, that the contemptors of the Druze or any initiatory movement, will call concealment.

The Druze tradition gives on this point the example of the initiate al Hallaj martyred in Baghdad in the 4th century for having proclaimed:

"I am the Truth" (ANA AL HAQQ), that is to say in mystical coded language "I am God".

Druze commentators accuse Al Hallaj of having revealed a secret in an "uncharitable" manner, since this act has led to crime those who have heard it, and found, according to the level of their weak Gnostic knowledge, unbearable, ungodly and condemnable.

4- FASTING is compulsory, as we know, during the period of a lunar month, Ramadan, every year; it is about not swallowing anything liquid or solid from sunrise to sunset; which, in semi-desert countries, and during the hot summer months, demands endurance worthy of respect.

Here too, the Druze interpret this commandment as an injunction to refrain from anything that distracts from the real purpose of existence, the search for union in God.

So the month of Ramadan, from this point of view, extends to the full length of the year.

5- The Pilgrimage: any believer, who has the financial means, must undertake it in Mecca at least once in his life, and comes back with the title of "Hajji", which has a connotation of seriousness and almost sanctified .

The Druze believe that the interior pilgrimage to the "House of God", the symbolic seat of Union in God.

They also take up the Muslim mystical traditions which, like Imam Mohammed Al Baqr, declare:

"The Black Stone (the Ka'ba in Mecca) around which we turn and touch out of respect is the symbol of the Supreme Leader, the Imam."

6- JIHAD, or fight for faith, has always been interpreted on two levels:

- fight the enemies of Islam, external for the Sunnis, but also internal for the Shiites, who want to slay those who supported the regimes opposed to Ali and the Imams.

- the internal fight against Evil.

For the Druze, by no means proselytes, it is about continual personal efforts to come closer to the knowledge of God.

7- WILAYA, finally, allegiance to the Higher Entities which incarnate during each cycle, aims to put into practice two obligations:

- in an Earth-Sky sense, it is to find and worship these Incarnate Powers,

- in an Earth-Earth sense, it means showing deep respect for all the brothers and sisters (Druzism is very egalitarian in terms of man-woman relations) who are faced with the same research, the same struggles, the same destinies .

For the initiates also, and only for them, one makes them understand that this initiation is a means of protecting the Druze religion against any denaturation; reserved for a small number (one to two out of ten), it is truly the basis of the religious organization of the whole community.

The Qur'anic verse "You did not know before what the Book or the Revelation" seems to apply to initiation which opens the way for an increasingly elaborate teaching:

the understanding of divine Oneness through four elements:

- mastery

- Distance from the material world, world of desire

- Comparative studies between esoteric texts and cosmic principles

- The experience of knowledge acquired individually, therefore incommunicable.

The initiate finally learns the role of reincarnation that would be described in the Koran (XVII, 51):

"Say:

Be stone or iron or whatever creature you can conceive of.

They will then say:

"Who will bring us back?"

Say, "He who first created you."

Sura XXVI "The Poets" is also cited in this connection.

Reincarnation constitutes, as we have seen, the basis of belief in Divine Unity (Tawheed):

"Your life is only one day old," says a Druze proverb, as it allows one to progress from bodily individualism towards Union with God ("There is no god but God").

The body is the means by which man progresses; he must therefore follow the adage "mens sana in corpore sans", therefore avoid alcohol, tobacco, drugs, all exciting in a word.

On the other hand, as soon as the soul leaves one body (apparent death), it enters another.

Successive and immediate reincarnations give the soul the opportunity to evolve in different environments and experiences.

A Druze must be able to get used to any earthly situation and experience them one after the other.

Recall that the Druze always reincarnates within the community, unlike non-Druze.

When he dies, we say:

"His soul has transmigrated".

Nevertheless, a Druze, who is unworthy, can be demoted in the body of a being whose level of esoteric knowledge will be lower, or, at the limit, to the most degrading social rank possible.

It is understood that most Druze take this belief very seriously.

The different degrees of Initiation

Composed of nine degrees, many initiates do not cross the first degree with difficulty.

For 100,000 Druze, it takes 5,000 initiates.

Those who are admitted to the first, second and third degree are Mutadaris then Rafik then Daï or Masters.

The highest rank is, as we have seen, that of Sheikh Aql.

Of course, this progression takes time, persistence and a lot of work.

The Mutadaris or Mubtad'i is not sure to be one day Rafik (Companion) and the latter will perhaps never be Dai (Master) and even less Cheikh Aql.

In the first degree, the Apprentice is subjected to a heavy fire of various questions, most often of a religious nature.

The Sheikh said to him, clapping his right hand on that of the Apprentice:

- Engage and promise me with the most sacred and the most inviolable oaths that you will not divulge our secret, that you will not give assistance against us to anyone.

When the Apprentice has taken the oath of allegiance, he will be able to access the initiation proper.

It is then that the seal of immortality is invoked upon him, referring to the four sources:

The first being the Intelligence, the second the Tâli or the Universal Soul, the third being the Natiq or the Enunciator and finally the fourth the Assas or the Foundation.

These four Sources where Elements are symbolized by the four elements:

- The Fire principle of heat (the test of Fire symbolizes the purification of the character).

- The Air, principle of fructification (the test of Air symbolizes intellectual purification).

- Water, the principle of coagulation (the Water test represents the purification of the candidate's spirit, a sort of initiatory baptism).

At the end of his races, he found this inscription:

"Whoever will have made these" Voyages ", alone and without fear, will be purified by Fire, Water, Air, and having been able to overcome the fear of death, having his soul prepared to receive the Light, he will have the right to leave the bosom of the Earth, and to be admitted to the revelation of the great mysteries ".

This first degree is the longest and most difficult of the degrees.

In the Second Degree, the proselyte learns that the Imams are the only ones who have received from God the mission to educate Muslims.

In the Third degree, he learns that the number of hereditary Imams is limited to 7, because as God created 7 heavens, 7 seas, 7 planets ... he appointed 7 revealed Imams: Ali, Hassan, Hussein, Zein al Abidin, Muhammad el Bakir, Jaafar al Sadiq and Ishmael his son as last and seventh.

The Fourth degree prepares the initiate for the Ways by making him know the 7 Prophets and legislators and their first vicars who are remembered:

Adam and Seth; Noah and Shem; Abraham and Ismail; Moses and Aaron; Jesus and Simon Peter; Muhammad and Ali; Muhammad son of Ishmael (the "Qaim el Zaman", that is to say, Head of this century).

After admitting the existence of another prophet after Muhammad, the Fifth degree makes him discover the law of numbers:

The importance of the number 7 (7 prophets, 7 successors, 7 planets, 7 heavens, 7 earths ...) as well as the number 12 corresponding to the 12 signs of the zodiac, to the 12 months of the year, to the 12 tribes of Israel, also the importance of the number 6: the 6 periods of the cycle of the prophecy from Adam to Muhammad each producing the spiritual forms. The number punctuating each period does not exceed the number 6 (if the creation of the Cosmos as it is said in a Koranic verse is 6 days ("He created the heavens and the earth in 6 days"), it is because the right limit (Hadd) of the Cosmos implies Matter and Form, Movement and Rest, Time and Space).

At the sixth degree, he engages further in philosophical ideas by comparing the doctrine of the prophets to that of philosophers such as Plato, Aristotle and Pythagoras.

At the Seventh degree of initiation he is taught that each of the founding prophets of a religion has an "Assas" (second) and that there are from the beginning of things two beings: one is higher (he gives), the other lower (he receives).
We thus recognize the two principles of all things: one male is fertile, the

other female is fertilized.

This dogma is also the object of the Eighth Degree: the proselyte is taught that, of these two, one is the sovereign governor of all that exists, and the other proceeds from him; that one of the two, which is the Preceding, has over the other, which is the Following, the same preeminence that the cause has over the effect.

In the Ninth degree, we teach that the Next, by his good behavior, reaches the degree of the Previous; that on earth, the Natek, by his good behavior, attains the degree of the Next, takes his place and occupies a rank equal to his; that the Assas, by its good conduct, attains a rank equal to that of Natek; that the Dai, by his good conduct, attains the degree of Assas and a rank equal to his, and that such is the course of things in the world in its different ages and successive periods.

In fact the initiatory formation of the 9 degrees is much more spiritual, more cosmic and mystical than what we have just enumerated.

It includes knowledge of the human body, the means to improve it, to master it and an "esoteric" medicine.

It also relates to spiritual exercises, "mystical" demonstrations, occult sciences (white magic, spiritualism, magnetism ...) etc ...

This is how we teach, among other things, all along the nine degrees:

The meaning of initiation, the meaning of numbers, spiritual force, the soul, the experimental development of psychic consciousness, breathing exercises, the law of the triangle, the existence of evil, the positive existence of good, the cosmos, some mystical experiences, dreams, the ego, the elimination of the ego, the elevation of the psychic self, the development of the psychic aura, the laws of the universe, the effects of light and of color, experiences of meditations, cycles of incarnation, the law of reincarnation, old age and death, rebirth and generation, control of the organs of the body, the mystery of fire and its place in the universe and in the human body, some alchemical experiences, action of thoughts on matter (magnetism), the real power of white magic, telepathy, self-control….

An overview of these spiritual exercises and of these "mystical" demonstrations was described by A.L. Rawson during his initiation in the 19th century among the Druze of Lebanon.

Freemason A.L Rawson was an American from New York, orientalist, influenced by Arab culture.

He was initiated among the Druze, then subsequently co-founded the Masonic Lodge "The Nobles of the Mystical Sanctuary".

He spent many years in the East and visited Palestine four times and visited Mecca.

He would have accompanied Madame Helena Blavatsky on her first trips to the Middle East.

The latter, as we have seen, was a Freemason and was initiated among the Druze.

It was a certain Greek from Cyprus, Hilarion Smerdis, who opened the doors to the Druze sanctuaries of Mount Lebanon to him.

This Hilarion Smerdis belonged to the masonic lodge "The Brotherhood of Luxor" just like another founding member of this Occult Lodge (which was composed of 7 members), Paulos Métamon.

Paulos Métamon was a Coptic adviser to the Viceroy of Egypt and Khedive Ismaïl Pasha, grandson of Mehemet Ali.

We know that Ismaïl Pasha studied in Paris, in particular at the Staff School and that he was initiated into Freemasonry by the French, in particular by the group of Ferdinand de Lesseps which mainly includes builders masons. He was Grand Master of the Grand Lodge of Egypt.

Paulos Métamon knew Madame Blavatsky during the many stays that the latter undertook in Egypt and he formed a solid friendship with her. He was said to be a magician and was feared and respected, and Egyptian officials went to see him secretly.

Initiated to the Druze religion, he would have been the depositary of the ancient Egyptian mysteries, in particular the secret of the real function of the Pyramids.

Coming back to A.L Rawson, he would have communicated to Madame

Blavatsky in 1877 an account of his experience and his initiation among the Druze of Lebanon.

This testimony is very interesting in itself since it describes two "Chambers" inside the Lodge: one which he calls "Gray Chamber" and the other "Chamber of Visions".

He relates on the one hand how his admission took place, the psychic exercises he underwent, his self-control, etc. in an underground which has a "Gray Room" hidden from the light of day, and only exposed in the smoky glow of a few lighted lamps, which resembles the "Cabinet of Reflections" at the Freemasons where the layman finds himself in 4 unusual states that he has difficulty enduring: loneliness, darkness, silence and stillness.

These states are conducive to confrontation with oneself.

The goal is to provoke a psychological shock, so as to "wake up" and invite meditation by the loss of landmarks and the acuity of the senses.

On the other hand from a "Chamber of Visions" where he had hallucinations!

These so-called psychic hallucinations are experienced by the person who is affected by them as an intrusion from the outside world into their own life.

It's as if another character has intruded into his consciousness, forcing him to act and think.

Here is her testimony to Madame Blavatsky:

Your note, asking me to give you an account of my initiation into a secret order among people commonly known as Druze, in Mount Lebanon, was received this morning.

I took, as you know perfectly well, an obligation at the time to hide in my own memory the greater part of the "mysteries" with the most interesting parts of the "instructions" so that what remains is not lost. no service to the public.

"My admission after a month (whereas as we saw above it takes several months), was made by special dispensation during which I was" guided "by a Sheikh, who served me cook, guide, interpreter and general servant, so that he can testify that I have strictly complied with the rules of food, ablutions and other matters.

"The initiates include both women and men, and the ceremonies are of such a special nature that both sexes are required to follow the ritual."

The "furniture" of the "prayer house" and the "vision room" is simple, and except for convenience, it can only be a strip of carpet.

In the "gray room" (the place is never named and is underground, not far from Beiteddin), there are rich decorations and precious old and dated furniture, the work of Arab goldsmiths, there are five or six centuries.

The day of initiation should be a day of continuous fasting, from sunrise to sunset in winter, or six hours in summer, and the ceremony is from beginning to end made up of a series of trials and temptations, calculated to test the candidate's endurance under physical conditions and mental pressure.

It is rare that the young man or the young woman succeeds in these "very difficult tests", because the neophyte will fail to pass certain tests.

In such a case, admission is extended for an additional year at the time of another invitation.

Choice pieces of cooked meat, salty soup, and other appetizing dishes, along with sherbet, coffee, wine, and water, are within reach of the neophyte who is left alone for a while with these tempting things in order to test his self-control.

For a hungry soul, the ordeal is severe.
But a more difficult test is when the seven priestesses withdraw, all but one, the youngest and the most beautiful, and the door is closed and barred outside, having warned the candidate that he will be left to his " reflections ", for half an hour.

Tired of the prolonged ceremonial, weak with hunger, parched with thirst, and a sweet reaction coming after the enormous effort to maintain his animal nature in submission, this moment of intimacy and closeness, and with looks that lend a double magnetic seduction to her words, begs him in low tones to "bless her".

Woe to him if he does!

A hundred eyes see it from secret peepholes, and it is only for the ignorant neophyte that there is the appearance of concealment and opportunity.

"There is no infidelity, idolatry, or any other really bad characteristic in the system."

They are confident of what once was a great form of natural worship, which was contracted under despotism in secret order, hidden from the light of day, and exhibited only in the smoky glow of a few lighted lamps, in a cave or a humid chapel underground.

The principles of their religious teachings are divided into 7 "Principles", which are these:

1- The unity of God, or the infinite unity of the divinity

2- The essential excellence of truth

3- The law of tolerance with regard to the opinion of all men and women

4- Respect for all men and women in terms of their character and conduct

5- Full submission to God's decrees on fate

6- Chastity of body, mind and soul

7- Mutual assistance in all conditions

These principles are neither printed nor written.

The main results of initiation appeared to be some sort of mental illusion or awake sleep, in which the neophyte saw, or thought he saw, images of people known to be absent, and in some cases thousands of miles away. .

I thought (or maybe it was my mind at work) that I was seeing friends and relatives that I knew at the time were in New York, while I was in Lebanon then.

How these results were produced I cannot tell.

They appeared in a dark room, when the "Sheikh" was speaking, "the Assembly" was singing in the next "room", and towards the end of the day, when I was tired of fasting, walking, talking, singing. , undressing, seeing great mental tension in resisting certain physical manifestations that result from appetites when they overcome willpower, and paying close attention to the passing scenes, hoping to remember them, so that I could have to be incapable of judging any of the new and surprising phenomena, and more particularly those seemingly magical appearances which have always excited my suspicion and mistrust.

I know the different uses of the magic lantern and the other devices, and I took care to examine the room where the "visions" appeared to me that very evening, the next day, and several times after, and I knew that, in my case, there was no use of machinery or any means other than the voice of the "guide" and the instructor.

Several times thereafter, at a great distance from the "room", identical or similar visions occurred as, for example, at the Hornstein Hotel in Jerusalem.

The daughter-in-law of a well-known Jewish merchant in Jerusalem is an initiate "sister", and can produce visions almost at will on anyone who will live strictly by the rules of the Order for a few weeks, more or less, depending on their nature. , raw or refined, etc.

"I am quite sure to say that the initiation is so special that it could not be printed in such a way as to instruct one who had not been 'worked' through the 'chamber'.

It would therefore be even more impossible to make a presentation of it as in Freemasonry.

"It is not necessary for me to say how certain notions of this people seem to perpetuate certain beliefs of the Ancient Greeks - like, for example, the idea that a man has two souls, and many others, for you have probably became familiar with them as you passed through the "upper house" and "lower house".

If I am wrong in assuming you are an "insider", please excuse me.

I am aware that friends often hide this "sacred secret" from each other; and even husband and wife can live - as it does in a family there - for twenty years together and yet neither of them know anything about the initiation of the other.

You have, without a doubt, good reasons for holding your own opinion.
Sincerely yours

The symbolism of the candle and the fire

Tamimi distinguishes in a candle (including its accessories) 5 letters, which is the emblem of the 5 joyful hidden: the Will, the Will, the Word, the Previous and the Next.

These five form the candle of the unitary doctrine:

the candlestick,

wax,

the wick,

and 4 and 5, the flame represented by the (coarse) wick and the subtle and light flame which occupies the higher end of the flame and which is red mixed with blue, which sometimes appears, sometimes disappears.

The subtle flame is the emblem of Intelligence associated with Hamza.

The thick flame represents the Soul.

The wax represents the Word.

The wick represents the Previous (Sabek)

The candlestick represents the Next (Tâli).

We know that the Jewish and Syrian theosophists, precursors of the alchemists, were philosophers of fire, they were attached to the Persian, Sabean and Phoenician traditions, professing for the Fire an almost unlimited cult and respect.

However, Fire played an essential role throughout the Middle Ages:

The Jewish cabalists declare that the hermetic or philosophical Fire is the universal miracle worker who presides over all transformations, this "philosophical" Fire, hidden in all bodies, invisible and present, was the primordial cause and its knowledge and "revelation" allowed the transmutation of the elements principle of alchemy.

The "Philosopher's Stone", the hermetic art of this noble regeneration of the bodies of nature, including the human body, was the center of research throughout the Middle Ages; Fire played a big role in his "generation".

Taking up the word of Hermes "what is above is like what is below"; "What applied to material bodies applied to spiritual bodies; metallic transmutation roughly corresponded to spiritual transmutation; the gross Fire was the reflection of a subtle "philosophical and divine" and divine Fire, transforming and generating of the spirit.

Numerology (the 3rd, 5th and 7th)

We note that in the Emerald Table and in the Treaty "Mukhtassar al Bayân", the number 3 finds its striking application:

Indeed, the Emerald Table begins with a Trinity:

It is true: Sensible truth corresponding to the physical world.

Without Lie: Opposition of the previous aspect. Philosophical truth, certainty corresponding to the metaphysical or moral world.

Very True: Union of the two preceding aspects, the thesis and the antithesis to constitute the synthesis. Intelligible truth corresponding to the divine world.

In the Treatise "Mukhtassar el Bayân", these are the Three kingdoms of nature:

The mineral kingdom

The plant kingdom

And the animal kingdom

The number 3 is of particular importance to Freemasons:

It represents the Delta or Triangle that we also find among the Druze.

Indeed, on the east wall of the Khalwa (Temple) there are symbols and figures which outline an emblem, which looks like a double triangle.

The vertex of the upper triangle is always at a very acute angle, while invariably the vertex of the lower triangle is almost at a right angle:

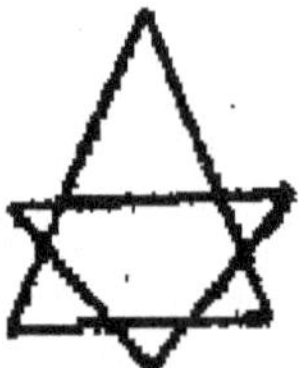

If we remove the two horizontal lines, which may have been added over the years, we obtain the Masonic emblem: the Square and the Compass.

The Compass is also present in the "Catechism of Druze".

Indeed to the question:

"What is the compass point?

The answer:

It is Hamza Ibn Ali.

In the book "Points and Circles" this point of the Compass means "the origin of all creatures".

In Persian, the point of the compass is the center around which everything revolves.

This reference of the Compass to Hamza who is called "Master of the Times" can be found in Freemasonry in the rank of Master by the expression "passage to another dimension of spirituality and the initiatory path".

Above this double triangle, we find an oval figure, which undoubtedly symbolizes the eye of God, which we find in Freemasonry "God who sees everything".

This reference to the triangle can also be found in the young Druze bride.

In fact, when she leaves the parental home, her mother gives her a triangular piece of paper on which prayers from the Book of Wisdom are written.

These symbols are also present in the Druze residences.

We also find strange forms that Druze women call "young brides" because of their distant resemblance to a human figure.

These figures never have two or four arms on each side, but always three or five.

Likewise the "3" appears in the Druze fraternal kiss.

Indeed, the Druze initiates mutually grasp each other's fingers and very quickly place their lips, 3 times, on the outer part of the hand of their religious brother.

The Accolade is given:

1-On the right cheek

2-On the left cheek

3-On the forehead

The Sign of Recognition:

In the Druze villages of Chouf (Lebanon) it is said that an Anglican priest, a Freemason, had bought a piece of land from a Sheikh Druze to build a Temple.

On the day of the signing of the deed of sale, Sheikh Druze went to shake hands with the priest Freemason by a special grip which was the same as the "Claw of the Master" in Freemasonry and that after putting a sacred tissue between the two hands as a form of blessing.
The number 3 is also present in the Catechism of the Druze:

At the question:

"What are the Feet of the Candlestick" (the candlestick on which we place the candle of the unitary religion)

A: These are the 3 Warnings

Q: Who are the 3 Warnings

R: They are John, Mark and Matthew

Q: For how many years have they been warning?

A: For 21 years (7x3), each of them Seven years

We also find the "5" to the question:

Who are the 5 Wise Virgins?

A: These are the Ministers of the Unitarian religion

Q: And what are the 5 Foolish Virgins

A: These are the Ministers of Law

(The Ministers of the Law those are those who enacted laws namely: Noah, Abraham, Moses, Issa (Jesus) and Mohammed. All are liars ".

Among the Freemasons:

The Masonic Accolade is threefold.

It is usually given on the right cheek, left cheek and right cheek, usually preceded by 3 hits with the right hand on the left shoulder.

3 steps, three lights, 3 hits for the battery and his Masonic age is 3 years!

In the lodges working in the Ecumenical Rite belonging to the Grand Orient Arabe, the Apprentice becomes familiar with the 3 letters I, A and O.

It is 3 letters animate the keys of Eastern Freemasonry.

Note that this number 3 occupies an important place both among the Druze and among the Freemasons but also in monotheistic religions.

Some examples:

- In Genesis, the first thing we learn is the presence of the 3 composed by Adam, Eve and the Serpent.

- In Christianity, baptism symbolically represents the purification of the person physically, mentally and spiritually.

We also find this in Islam in ablutions.

Also the Trinitarian doctrine actually represents the three stages of human growth and development:

God the Father represents the dominant will to submit to the Creator; the Son represents the state of mind or consciousness that is formed after the will is manifested and finally the Holy Spirit can be interpreted to the spirit that dominates the human being.

We also find the importance of the number 3 in the Gospels:

* Jesus lifted up the widow's son by pressing him 3 times (Luke 7,11).

* Destroy this Temple and in 3 days I will raise it (John 2,19)

* Jesus was resurrected on the 3rd day after his death.

* Saint Peter denied Jesus 3 times
etc ..

and in Islam:

* the angel Gabriel asked the Prophet Muhammad to read 3 times, it was only at the 3rd injunction that the Prophet said and what should I read? And could recite the words that the angel Gabriel whispered to him!

* the prayer called Salat el Maghreb (sunset) is composed of 3 raka'at and alludes to the resurrection of the mind, the moral and the spiritual.

The number 5

The five-colored star which represents the five universal principles of the Druze is similar in its components to that used in Freemasonry.
"The five-pointed star or Pentalpha, the most important symbol, was the sign of recognition of the Pythagorean school. (...) The members of this school made correspond to each of the vertices of the figure one of the letters of the word Health (in Greek). (...): Each of the letters composing the word is a "Pythagorean letter".

Professor Sami Makarem, author of the book "The Druze Faith" refers to this number by writing:

"In the age of deep knowledge and deep learning, the reform of the Druze faith should be directed towards understanding the principles and foundations of the deep faith, towards the true meaning of God: the Lahut and the Nasut, towards the "Aql and the Cosmic Five", principles of existence, (each point being represented by a point on the star Druze) with the difference between the origin (ibda '), the creation (Khalq) and the 'emanation (fayd, inbi'ath), to humanity as such, to the truth, unlike Islam (surrender or peace) and Iman (belief) and Tawhid (certainty), for form and matter, soul and body, virtue and vice, knowledge and gnosis, life and death, religion and science, physics and metaphysics, individual and society, paradise and hell, in the sense of theophany and occultation, in the true sense of freedom: the difference between freedom and free will, to name just a few examples of the main challenges them of the Druze faith ".

So we see that Druze doctrine and symbolism is based on Five points of communion, represented by their Five-pointed star.

But it is the number 7 which occupies a very important place among the Druze.

As we have seen according to them, the world has known 7 great prescribers of laws, 7 great priests and 7 major prophets, each inspired by the 7 first spirits.

Hamza's Moral Law is summed up in 7 chapters.

The 7 characteristics of the Unitarians are:

1 - Veracity in speeches

2 - Loyalty to his religious brothers

3 - Renunciation of the worship of idols

4 - Distance from Satan and his supporters

5 - Belief in the divinity of Hakim

6 - Consent

7 - Satisfaction

At the question:

Q: "What is prescribed for you?

A: The veracity in the speeches, the worship of Hakim and the rest of the 7 precepts.

Q: And what are some painful observances for you that Lord Al Hakim has dispensed with and abrogated?

A: These are the 7 Bonds

(These are the 7 obligations imposed by force by law and which Al Hakim abrogated; they constitute the bases of the Muslim religion: the 2 Chahâdat, fasting, prayer, legal alms, the pilgrimage to Mecca, holy war and submission to religious leaders).

But the most interesting point in this combination of 7, regarding the relationship between the Druze world and Freemasonry, is their common belief in the influence of the 7 stars.

(As we have seen, the Great Initiates of the Druze Mysteries practice the occult art of astrology).

This star-based divination is essentially limited to the movements and influences of what they call the 7 planets.

According to their belief, the fixed stars have nothing to do with the affairs of this world, and for this reason they have abandoned the study of these constellations.

They focus their attention on the following:

Saturn, Jupiter, Mars, Venus, Mercury, the Sun and the Moon.

These 7 celestial bodies, they say, were specially created by the original 7 spirits, under the influence of the Great Architect of the Universe.

Each is the home of one of the 7 spirits, from where they order and regulate everything that happens in this world.

Prosperity, adversity, success and failure, happiness, misfortune, life and death, would flow completely and directly from the auspicious or contrary influence of the 7 spirits of these 7 heavenly bodies.

Now, would it not be possible to see this mystical Druze belief in astrology somehow related to the 7 stars of the Masonic tradition?

Masonry historians frequently have recourse to a few quotes from authors of operative masonry (builders) such as Philippe Delorme (1515-1570) who said:

"There are 7 parts in the architecture:

1 - The walls

2 - The doors

3 - The fireplaces

4 - Windows

5 - The area and the pavement

6 - Floors

7 - The covers

The whole being implemented with a necessary harmony and an indispensable symmetry.

We should not find this remark strange, touching the 7 things necessary for the construction and the conversation of a main building, since this Great Architect of the Universe, Almighty God, represented it to us and showed it to us when he created the 7 wandering stars called planets, like matter or rather the form of the establishment, perfection and conversation of the so admirable building of this lower world.

So that one of its aforesaid planets failed in the competition of this occult harmony which maintains in good harmony the elements of discord, the aforesaid building of this small world would be uninhabitable and useless.

By which, not without cause, Mercury Trismegistus does not seem to have written correctly that these 7 planets were created and ordered by God, as sustenance, rectors and governors, after him, of the lower and sensitive world, 7 columns which support and establish, after God, the state and vigor of this little kingdom and university of the lower world ".

Philippe Delorme then explains that in his kingdom:

1-Saturn represents Agriculture

2-Jupiter Justice

3-March the Gendarmerie

4-Venus the Love of the Lord for her vassal

5-Mercury Trade

6-the Sun the King

7-the Moon the common people, the Craftsmen

Oswald Wirth (1860-1943) sought a connection between the duties of officers in a Masonic Lodge and the astrological planetary symbolism he presents as follows:

1- the Venerable corresponds to Jupiter (the ruler of the heavens because wisdom dominates in him)

2- the Senior Deacon to Mars (the fierce god, whose rigor and strength must be inflexible)

3- the Junior Warden to Venus (the sweet and beautiful)

4- the Speaker to the Sun (guardian of Masonic law)

5- the Secretary to the Moon (reflection of the Sun, he faithfully records everything that emanates from the Speaker's board)

6- The Expert to Saturn (the prudent god, who stands in dark places)

7- the Master of Ceremonies to Mercury (the messenger of the gods)

Likewise, Freemasonry constantly refers to progressions "3, 5 and 7".

The first use of this progression can be seen in connection with the composition of the Lodge:

Q: Where have you been received?

A: In a just and perfect Lodge

Q: What does it take for a Lodge to be just and perfect?

A: 3 rule it, 5 compose it, 7 make it just and perfect

Q: Who are these 7?

A: The Venerable, the Senior and Junior Deacon, two FellowCraft and Entered-Apprentice.

This mention is one of the mandatory points of the opening of the works.

We cannot, in principle, proceed with this opening if this number 7 is not reached.

The number 7 was seen in the Middle Ages as the expression of totality, of perfection.

The sages attributed a high idea of perfection to the septenary.

The early Greeks called it septa or venerable.

Cicero, initiated in the science of numbers, assures us, in the dream of Scipio, that there is hardly anything of which this number is not the knot.

It symbolizes, in the mastery, the moral chain which unites Masonic science to civilization and to the happiness of mankind.

Thus in Masonic instruction at the grade of Master, to the question:

"How old is a Master"

A: 7 years and over

Q: Why do you say and more? And what does the number 7 mean?

A: This is to express that he knows not only the mysteries of mastery, but also those that could be derived from it.

The number 7 signifies the 7 planets, the 7 metals, the 7 primitive colors, the 7 musical notes ...

Other symbols are common to the Druze and Freemasonry such as the Pyramids.

In the Druze catechism the question:

"What is this building in Egypt called Pyramids?"

A: These Pyramids, our Lord built them in his wisdom.

Q: What wisdom is there in this?

A: It is to deposit there the documents and covenants that our Lord took from humans to keep there until the day of his second return. "

Gematria and Kabbalistic Analysis.

It is Hamza who in his Epistle VI uses gematria in the formula "Bismillaahir-Rahmaanir-Rahîm" (In the name of God, The Most Gracious, The Most

Merciful) to define the number of Hudud and an esoteric and kabbalistic analysis around the number 7 and the letter Alif (A) of the profession of Islamic faith "La Illaha Illa Allahu, Muhammadu Rasûlu Ilahi" (There is no deity except Allah; Muhammad is the envoy of Allah).

a- the "Basmalah"

For Hamza the number of Hudud is supposed to correspond to the numerical value of the letters of Bismillah.

In Freemasonry in the Ecumenical Rite practiced by Lodges belonging to the Grand Orient Arab, as well as most other rites such as the Scottish Rite, the first letter that the future Apprentice / Mubtad'i spells out is the B or Beth in Hebrew or BÂ in Arabic, since it is the first letter he spells of the word BOAZ

We notice that this letter which "begins" the initiation of the Mourid in its long journey, is the first letter of the Torah, which begins the word Berèshit, "At the Beginning", and in Islam "Begins" most of the suras: " Bismillah al Rahmân al Rahîm "(In the name of God, The Most Gracious, The Most Merciful).

Prophet Muhammad is credited with saying:

"It is from the letter Bâ that the being has manifested".

Indeed, the existing things appeared from the Bâ, the first letter of Bismillah al Rahmân al Rahîm (in the name of God, Most Gracious, Most Merciful), which opens the First Surah "AL FÂTIHA".

Bâ is the letter which, in alphabetical order, comes immediately after Alif; now the Alif corresponds to the Essence of Allah.

The Ba coming second corresponds to the First Intellect (al Aql al Awal) which is the first created by Allâh.

Through his readings, the "Mourid" / Apprentice became familiar, among other things, with "Gematria".

He thus had the correspondence between the letters of the Arabic alphabet and the numbers:

Numerology chart says "Abjad" of the alphabet.

Lettre	Nombre
ALIF	1
BA	2
JIM	3
DAL	4
HA	5
WAU	6
Z	7
HH	8
TT	9
YA	10
KAF	20
LAM	30
MIM	40
NUN	50
SIN	60
AYN	70
FA	80
SD	90
QAF	100
R	200
SH	300
T	400
TH	500
KH	600
DZ	700
DH	800
TZ	900
GH	1000

Each of the 28 letters of the Arabic alphabet (alif to Yé) has a numerical value, therefore signifying a number.

And in the formula Bismillaahir-Rahmaanir-Rahîm there are 19 letters.

When we add the numerical values of each of these nineteen letters, we get a total of 786 (Seven hundred and eighty six).

786 is thus used to symbolically evoke Bismillaahir-Rahmaanir-Rahîm.

The grammatical value of "Bismillah" corresponds to the number "786".

Now 786 is 7 + 8 + 6 = 21 which are the 21 letters of "Bismil-lâhi Rahmâni Rahîm" in Arabic.

The total count of the letters that compose them is always the same: it is the number 19

This number is underlined in the following verse of the Quran (74:30):

"They are nineteen to watch over it"

as well as in Epistle 13 of Hamza entitled "The unveiling of the Truths":

"The first dignitary is the Soul, which has 12 Arguments in the Islands and 7 Propagandists for the 7 climates, which is why he says:

"Its Supervisors are 19 in number."

b- The esoteric and kabbalistic analysis around the number 7 and the letter Alif (A) of the Islamic profession of faith:

"La Illaha Illa Allahu, Muhammadu Rasûlu Ilahi".

[…] The First Part of the profession of faith (La Illaha Illa Allahu) consists of two statements, which refer to the Advance (Sabek) and the Following (Tali); it has four words designating the two Bases (Assas) and the two Foundations; it has 7 syllables referring to the 7 Enunciators, 7 Trustees (Awsiya), 7 days, 7 heavens, 7 earths, 7 mountains and 7 spheres; it totals twelve letters, symbol of the Twelve Arguments (Hugag) linked to the Foundation.

The Second Part of the profession of faith (Muhammadu Rasûlu Ilahi) is divided into 3 words which have the emblem of the 3 Ministers: the Natek, the Tali who is above him, and the Sabek, who is above all.
It is divided into 6 parts which indicate the 6 Nateks. It has 12 letters which indicate the 12 Hodgas opposed to those of Assas. Thus there are 2 times 12 signs and 7 planets that they govern, 7 lands, 7 climates and 12 islands.

But the primitive source of the whole Universe is one, it is the cause of the causes. It is he whom they know under the name of Sabek he is the source of rest and cold, the Tali is the source of heat and movement.

Iblis the cursed came out of the Sabek before the Tali, he is subtle and spiritual, he was obedient to his creator. But he manifested jealousy, he claimed primacy so his spiritual substance became a being opposed to the Sabek, he manifested his enmity, he argued against his creator, and was named

Haret, so the Tali came out of the Sabek and the Tali became the origin of the whole Universe.

These two were produced the Natek and Assas. The Sabek manifested its cold and its rest, the Tali its heat and movement, the Natek the drought, and the Assas the movement, the 4 elements were formed, and the 7 planets as well as the 12 signs were formed.

Among the 12 signs each division of 3 signs has a different nature from each of the other divisions partially formed of 3 signs so that the world is governed by 4 elementary principles.

Likewise, there are 4 spiritual elements, as we have already said.
But the Creator has nothing to do with all of this and is well raised above any definitions of him.

The 7 planets together form 28 letters, so that the Gnostics can see clearly that all these things which are counted by the number 7 only indicate the same thing and have only the same meaning.

These names are Saturn, Jupiter, Mars, the Sun, Venus, Mercury and the Moon, whose letters are 28 in number.

From the first signs that begin the year, that is to say from Aries, which is the Sabek, to the one that corresponds to it, that is to say to Libra which is the Natek , there are 7 signs namely Aries, Taurus, Gemini, Cancer, Leo, Virgo and Libra and the letters of which these names are composed form the number 28.

All human conduct, prosperity, and setbacks are regulated by the Moon, and the Moon only completes its course in 28 stations (1).

Since the month of Muharram in Rajab which enjoys the same prerogatives as Muharram, 7 months ago, Muharram is the emblem of the Sabek, he is the beginning of the year and the first of the month.

Rajab is the emblem of the Tali: he immediately joins with Chaabane and Ramadan. These two months are the emblem of Natek and Assas.

Muharram who represents the Sabek is alone and separated from the other privileged months.

But Rajab is joined with two other privileged months, just as the Tali is immediately joined with Natek and Assas.

From the month of Muharram to that of Rajab, 7 months ago.

Likewise the Sabek has 6 Ministers. The first is the Tali, Courage, Victory, Imagination, Natek and Assas whose names form 28 letters.

Behind Mouharram, Safar, Rabia (1st), Rabia (2nd), Djumadi (1st), Djumadi (2nd),

Rajab form 28 letters.

The names of the 7 days of the week: Sunday, Monday, Tuesday, Wednesday, Thursday, Friday and Saturday also form 28 letters.

Similarly also the 7 Natek: Adam, Noah, Abraham, Moses, Jesus, Mohammad, and Saïd (2) also have 28 letters.

The 7 confidants (Al Awsiya) whose names are Seth, Sem, Ismaïl, Joshua, Simeon, Ali and Qaddah (3) also have 28 letters.

We also distinguish in the Koran 7 types of writings: what abrogates, what is abrogated, what is clear, what the meaning is obscure, the stories, the relationships, and the comparisons. They are also read according to 7 variants.

We go around the Ka'ba 7 times.

The man's length is 7 spans measured with his hand; his width is also 7 spans (4). It has 7 openings in the face.

There is also an infinity of other things that can be counted by 7 that cannot be understood in this writing, all of which are the emblem of the 7 Imams, the 7 Natek, and the 7 confidants.

They all have for principle a single Being who is himself a creature subject to his creator and not the adorable Being.

It is in this sense that it is said: "Your creation was made, and your resurrection will be done as if you were only one person".

This person is the Sabek, emblem of the Dai, because he will hold the Imam's mission.

In an identical way, the existence of the letter Lâm in the first part of the profession of faith:

The Illaha can be reduced to the letter Alif (5).

In the same way the Lâm curves back up towards the Alif and the Alif which is in the Lâm is the emblem of the Imam (5).

The second Alif is the emblem of the Tali. And the Lâm is the emblem of the Natek because the Natek receives a mission from the Tali and it is from him that he draws his instruction.

The third Alif which is in the word Illa holds the rank of the Sabek since he holds the fourth rank among the Ministers.

It is the emblem of Hoddjah, Dai and Ma'dhun.
The Alif who is in the Lâm has only one Minister who is the Tali.

Just as the Dai depends only on the Imam, and the Natek on the Tali, but the Sabek has authority over all the Ministers.

So it is with the Alif of the word Allah. The two Lâm who are near him indicate the Natek and the Tali, while the final Hâ has a rank similar to that of Assas.

Therefore, when we say: "There is no God except Allah", he removes all these terms from their usual meaning and applies them to his Assas.

Then he forced them to say: Muhammad Rasûl Allah (Muhammad is the Messenger of God).

This second part of the profession of faith is composed of 3 words because it is the 3rd from the Sabek.
It is made up of 3 syllables, because it is the 6th of the Nateks.

It has 12 letters which designates its 12 Hodgas which belong to the outer law, just as Assas has 12 Hodgas which belong to the inner law.

So after considering the Sabek, Tali, Assas, Imam, and Hodga, we prove that they are all servants, united and mated with each other, but the adorable being is different from all.

We have also learned by the grace of Our Lord that the Hâ of which we have already spoken, that is to say the one who ends and ends the word Allah, that the two Lâm and Alif. He is therefore the last, who comes in 4th position, the one who completes the power.

Therefore, we say of him what we do not say of any other dignitary, in particular that he is the Mahdi, bearer of this supreme name: Abu al Qâ'im.

This name only occurs to the most eminent of the dignitaries, the one who is their supreme limit, just as the letter Hâ is the term of the profession of faith: La Illaha Illa Allah.

[…]

Explanations and Comments:

(1) The time it takes for the Moon to return to the same point in its orbit, knowing that the synodic revolution of the Moon takes approximately 29 days.

This brings us back to the Ikhwan el Safa theory of prosperous and harmful Conjunctions.

(2) Saïd Ibn al Hussein, nicknamed Obaydallah al-Mahdi (881-934) is as we saw in the first chapter the first Fatimid Caliph.

(3) The controversy hostile to the Fatimids maintains that they have no right to the Imamate, since they would not descend from Ali and Fatma, but from a certain al-Kaddah, an impostor of obscure origin . This thesis could be of Qarmatian origin.

(4) Provided of course that he extends his arms horizontally. It makes us think of the Vitruvian Man, the famous drawing by Leonardo da Vinci.

(5) The interpretation of Alif among the Sufis:

Alif corresponds to the Supreme Name, to Allah!

This is the First Created from whom the degrees of the rest of the universe proceed.
All the letters need Alif, while he can do without them.

Indeed none of the other numbers can do without it, as we will demonstrate below:

If we take the following:

the Bâ, it is composed of (b + a), it will be the same for the others, take for example the Nûn it is composed of (n + w + n; or in the w, which is called Wâw = w + a + w, and we finally find an Alif.

It is the same for the Lâm: It could not exist without the Alif, since it enters into its composition.

Whoever knows the exoteric of Alif and its esoteric, has reached the mystical degree of the Truths (Siddîqûn).

Alif is composed of A = 1; L = 30 and F = 80 which gives 111 according to the Numerology table called "Abjad" of the alphabet.

c- The Druze filiation of the Rite of Memphis-Misraïm

In the ritual of the Constitution and the Installation of a Respectable Lodge at the Rite of Memphis-Misraïm, the Grand Master, after having proceeded to the Ceremony of the various Delegations which came to bring their fraternal support, proceeds to a quick account of the history and the origins of the Rite of Memphis-Misraïm, resulting from the Rite of Misraïm (created in Venice in 1788), associated with the Primitive Rite (1779), then, and by Garibaldi, united with the Rite of Memphis (1815).

He recalls that the latter, founded by scholars who participated in the Egyptian Campaign (1), all members of the old initiatory Obediences of the Philaleths, the Philadelphians and the Hermetic Rite (Illuminati of Avignon), was formed on traditions and of the lineages they had brought back from Egypt and Lebanon.

And to add that:

"Gérard de Nerval, in his *Voyage en Orient*, demonstrated that there existed traditions and a secret society within the Druze, resulting from the medieval Fellow Craft having accompanied the Crusaders, and later associated with the Templars.

Also, the role that the Caliph Al Hakim had played in the maintenance of the Gnostico-Egyptian traditions, which were still in force in his time in Cairo.

Thus, the Rite of Memphis is indeed resulting, thanks to Gaspard Monge, Larret, etc .., of this survival of the ancient Egyptian mysteries within the Druze Masonry.

If we doubted it, it would suffice for us to remember that the National Library in Paris has Gnostic manuscripts written in the 12th century in Damascus itself.

Finally, it is not thus without reason that the Masons who constituted the Rite of Memphis chose for their Lodges and Chapters names such as "The Druze Reunited", or "The Knights of Lebanon", nor one of the high grades of the Rite are called "Sublime Day" which is one of the secret grades of the Druze initiates ".

(1) The speculative front row in Egypt

The first lodge appeared in Alexandria in 1748.

But with the bubbles of excommunications of the Freemasons in 1749, like Turkey, Freemasonry could not develop, especially since the investigation of the representative of the Greek community -Catholic (Melkite) of Cairo it was decided to propagate in 1751 the Bull of Pope Benedict XIV translated into Arabic, Armenian and Greek languages!

It was with Bonaparte's expedition in 1798 that military lodges were introduced to Egypt.

Military lodges to which belonged Catholics, Protestants, Orthodox and Jews soon joined by the Muslims with the Mamelukes.

The first known lodge "La Loge ISIS"

In fact the first lodge established on Egyptian soil was founded by the French General Jean-Baptiste Kléber (1753 - 1800) and this just after Napoleon's return to France.

Born in Strasbourg Jean-Baptiste Kleber was General-in-Chief of the Army of the Rhine before becoming the General-in-Chief of the Army of Egypt during Bonaparte's expedition.

Freemason like several officers who accompanied Napoleon, he founded in Alexandria the Lodge "ISIS" of which he was Venerable Master.

This lodge, which had adopted the slogan of the French Revolution "Liberté-Égalité-Fraternité", only included a few Egyptians.

Most of the members who joined were from close relatives of Bonaparte and French officers.

The "Isis" lodge did not last long, however.

It disappeared just after the assassination of General Kléber in 1800 and dissolved in 1801, two years after its creation.
During the same year, the Lodge "Saint John of Scotland of the Great Sphinx" was created in Egypt.

This lodge was mainly composed of French artists (painters, engravers, architects.).

The "Brothers" of the lodge brought back with them to Paris, 60 moldings of Egyptian bas-reliefs.

These bas-reliefs have contributed to expanding the collection of antiquities of the Scottish Philosophical Mother Lodge.

This Respectable Lodge in the Orient of Paris in the Grand Orient of France had as Venerable Master Claude-Antoine Thory who had installed an initiatory museum aimed at demonstrating that Freemasonry was the heir to the Egyptian Mysteries.

The Lodge "The Disciples of Memphis"

Another lodge will also see the light of day in 1799.

It was also founded by officers of Bonaparte's army, all members of the Grand Orient de France and disciples of the Rite of Narbonne (rite founded in France on April 19, 1780) and who had contact with Druze initiates during the Napoleon's campaign.

Seduced by the latter, they renounced the filiation of the Grand Lodge of England and created in Cairo the Lodge "The Disciples of Memphis" in accordance with the tradition of the Rite of Narbonne.

In 1814, a certain Samuel Honis, born in Egypt and member of the lodge "The Disciples of Memphis" where he was initiated, came to France and settled in Montauban.

On May 23, 1815, he founded the lodge "The Disciples of Memphis" which later became the Mother Lodge of the Rite of Memphis and which had in 1816 as Grand Hierophant Marconis de Nègre.

Samuel Honis will subsequently create several lodges in Egypt including the "MENES" lodge at the Rite of Memphis.

Another lodge was to be created on August 28, 1799 in Cairo, the same day General Bonaparte left Egypt, the Lodge "Les Vrais Amis Réunis".

This lodge will meet until October 1801 and will give birth to the lodge of Toulon which bears its name to this day.

d- Hudud and Landmark

The Hudud (in Arabic al-Hudud) means "the borders" where "limits" corresponding to the Landmark among the Freemasons.

Indeed, the biblical meaning of the word landmark is also "the border" or "limits".

This word appears 240 times in the Old Testament and it seems to be from the same root as the word Geval which is the Hebrew name for the city called in Greek Byblos.

Byblos was the center of a Phoenician kingdom, the land of the guiblites, from which came the masons and stonemasons who were employed in the construction of Solomon's Temple in Jerusalem.

From this comes the word gibelin to which Masonic rituals still give the meaning of "excellent mason" today.

These "Limits" or "Laws" or "Regulations" were defined on the one hand by Hamza among the Druze and by Anderson among the Freemasons.

The Druze, on the other hand, borrowed this word Hudud from the Koran.

Indeed, the Prophet Mohammad, after having established some laws relating to guardianship and inheritance said:

"These are the Hudud of Allah ... and whoever rebels against Allah and his messenger and transgresses his Hududs, He will cause him to enter into the fire to abide therein eternally" (Sura 4, verse 17).

We also find this warning or intimidation, among the Freemasons who, for their part, refer as we have seen to the Old Testament where it is said:

"Cursed be he who moves the boundaries (Hudud) of his neighbor". (Deuteronomy 27,17).

where "Do not take away the ancient Landmarks which your fathers set up" (Proverbs 22,28).

What are the Hudud among the Druze

Hamza systematized the Druze religion and presented himself as the direct human link with the One.

He then established a hierarchy of universal principles, or al-Hudud, which would span the distance between the One and the mass of Druze believers.

Each Hadd (singular of Hudud) had a human counterpart among the contemporaries of al-Ḥakim.

-1) Hamza himself became the first principle, or Hadd, Universal Intelligence (al-Aql)

2) al-Aql generated the Universal Soul (al-Nafs), embodied in Ismaïl ibn Muḥammad al-Tamimi.

3) The Word (al-Kalima) emanates from al-Nafs and manifests itself in the person of Muḥammad ibn Wahb al-Qurashi.

4) The fourth successive principle is the Previous (al-Sabek, or Right [al-Janaḥ al-Ayman]), embodied in Salama ibn Abd al-Wahhab aL-Samirri.

5) The fifth is the Following (al-Tali), or Left wing [al-Janāḥ al-Aysar]), personified by al-Muqtana Bahaeddine.

Each of these principles, the real Hudud, also had false counterparts, in turn embodied by various contemporaries of al Hakim.

The tension between the two sets of Hudud represented the conflict of Good and Evil in the world.

These Five Cosmic Principles are emanations from God, the ONE.

These are the 5 Superior Ministers.

The Lower Ministers are:

1) The Application or Ayoub, son of Ali

2) The Opening or Rifaa, son of Abd al Warith

3) The Phantom or Muhsin, son of Ali

then come the Daïs, Ma'dhun, Mocasers, or Nakibs.

Other Principles that we have already seen: the seven compulsory precepts to follow and which are:

1- not to lie (therefore not to steal, not to kill, not to be adulterous)

2- love his brothers in the faith and come to their aid

3- not believing "in your soul" in other religions

4- not to reveal the mysteries of our Lord

5- renounce the "Rival"

6- be subject to the divine will,

7- be strong and resigned to happiness as well as to adversity.

Landmarks (Hudud) among the Freemasons

The Landmarks constitute for the Freemasons the main fundamental principles of their particular system of morals, which were adopted by the founders of the first Grand Lodge from 1717 because they were considered essential.

The sources of Landmarks in the Masonry Craft are the Old Charges. These sources highlight a fundamental fact:

Masonry works to the glory of God, recognized under his attribute of

Creator and designated under the name of Grand Architect of the Universe.

The Anderson Constitutions of 1723 of the speculative period take up the fundamental Landmarks and use the general theme of the construction of Solomon's Temple as a symbolic figure of spiritual realization.

In this sense, there is no break with the operative period, only the material changes, we go from stone to man as a material that must be worked in order to be brought into conformity with God's plan, Great Architect of the Universe.

Landmarks are inseparable from:

1) Faith in God and in his revealed will

2) Moral behavior in accordance with the covenant with God

3) Respect for the law as a sign of freedom

4) The practice of fraternity and charity as rules of the trade.

This is what allowed the United Grand Lodge of England to define the criteria on which the regularity of a Masonic power is based, and therefore of all those which come under its Obedience.

Here are the terms and conditions:

1) The regularity of its origin, that is to say that each Grand Lodge will have

been created by a duly recognized regular Grand Lodge and by three or more regularly constituted Lodges.

2) That faith in the Great Architect of the Universe and in his revealed will will be an essential condition for the admission of members.

3) That all initiates should lend their obligation to the Volume of the Sacred Law or with their eyes fixed on this open book through which is expressed the revelation from above, to which the individual who has just been initiated is, on his conscience, irrevocably bound.

4) That a Grand Lodge and the blue lodges placed under its authority will be exclusively composed of men, and that each Grand Lodge will not maintain any Masonic relationship of any kind whatsoever with mixed lodges or with bodies which admit women as members.

5) That the Grand Lodge will exercise sovereign jurisdiction over the Lodges under its control, that is to say that it will be a responsible, independent and fully autonomous body, possessing a unique and uncontested authority over the profession or the symbolic degrees (registered apprentice, journeyman in the trade and master mason) placed under its jurisdiction, and that it will in no way be subordinate to a Supreme Council or any other Masonic power claiming control or supervision of these degrees, nor will it share his authority with that Council or that power.

6) That the three great lights of Freemasonry (that is to say the Volume of the Sacred Law, the Square and the Compass) will always be exhibited during the work of the Grand Lodge or the lodges placed under its control, the main

of these lights being the Volume of the Sacred Law.

7) That religious and political discussions will be strictly prohibited in the lodge.

8) That the principles of ancient Landmarks, customs and uses of the trade will be strictly observed.

On reading these fundamental criteria (the "Basic Principles"), regular Masonry declares itself resolutely theistic.
The Great Architect of the Universe is neither a symbol nor a vague philosophical concept, but the Creator God, ultimate cause who is at the origin of the manifested world and who makes an alliance with man in the sacred texts of religions revealed.
Masonic regularity here testifies to a desire to bring together men of all faiths who have in common to believe and accept revelation from above.

It was on these foundations of Universality that speculative masonry was built at the beginning of the 18th century.

Coming back to the "Basic Principles", it remains nonetheless that this formulation more in keeping with the spirit of the first version of Anderson's Constitutions published in 1723 does indeed consider "the Supreme Being" as the "Creative Principle" of the Universe, "the Unique", "the ONE" from which all things proceed to use the neo-Platonic terminology dear to Plotinus and the Druze.

e- John the Evangelist among the Druze and the Freemasons

1- Among the Druze

The unitary doctrine among the Druze is still called the Word or the Word, the Word of Truth, the Word united to the Messiah.

The real Messiah is Hamza.

This is how Bahaeddine Al Moqtana defines it in a treatise where he says, referring to John the Evangelist (Bahaeddine, as we will see, often mentions John in his writings):

"My intention is not to fight the real dogmas of the sect of Christians; but I obeyed the command which was given to me to give to the religious, virtuous men who are among them, the true meaning of the divine precepts; to let them know, through texts of the Gospel, the faults they have committed; to show them that they were mistaken in their idea of it, and which is the object of their belief; that while they were called to recognize the real existence of the Creator, of the adorable being, they reduced it to a real nothingness, and they did not fully understand the meaning of the Word united to the Messiah, so as to know all its excellence.

The Messiah said to his Apostles:

"In truth I say to you, that any man who will keep my word will never see death (1).

He did not say:

"Whoever does the works that I do will never see death."

This word is the true doctrine of the unitary religion [...]

(1) Gospel of Saint John, 8, 51

[…] Wake up therefore, Christians, for already he who sowed rejoiced when he saw the reaper arrive (1); already the presence of the Word of truth has served as a testimony against the unbeliever and the infidel… and, as the Lord said, lift up your eyes and consider the lands which are already white, and the time of harvest is very close (2).

(1) and (2) Gospel of Saint John 4, 35 and 36

The Messiah said again:

"Because of these terrible days and their great number, charity will be weakened and will cease in the hearts of many men; but he who waits patiently to the end will obtain eternal life, and Jesus will proclaim the gospel of the kingdom.

It will be so in everyone, it will serve as a testimony against all peoples; then the hour will come.

So wake up, Church of Christians, who are in fluctuation and foolish uncertainty about your religion, and consider these words that he has said, that Jesus will publicly announce the gospel of the kingdom, that it will be so in everything. the world, and will be a testimony against all peoples. For you ungodly men, you did not pay attention to these nine years during which he publicly announced the Gospel of the kingdom (1), and you were stunned in this regard; you refused to recognize them, and your minds were clouded with a kind of drunkenness. [...]

(1) The 9 years would begin after Hakem's disappearance.

We know that Bahaeddine Al Moqtana was a "dai" and that he exercised his functions in Syria by proselytizing.

This is how he met the Christians and got to know their religion perfectly and through three writings he was able to address them.

The first writing dated 1028, Bahaeddine Al Moqtana is addressed to Constantine, Emperor of Christians and to all the Christian hierarchy (Patriarchs, Bishops, Priests etc.) in these terms:

"Assembly of Saints, if you receive what John Bouche d'Or, the apostle, wrote in his gospel; if you firmly believe what is received by common accord by all the leaders of your religion; if you put faith in the three hundred and eighteen who spoke by the inspiration of the holy spirit, in Constantinople; if you recognize as true the symbol of your faith, that all Christian sects, notwithstanding the diversity of their opinions, always recite in their liturgies and their sacrifices: in this case, societies of the saints, pay me attention, and consider what recite your ministers at each mass, and the expectation you are in for the coming of Jesus Christ who must come to save all men ...

This symbol of your faith is the one that has been drawn up unanimously by the heads of Christendom, by the principal among those who practice the ceremony of the waters of baptism, by the patriarchs, the metropolitans, the bishops and the priests, who have spoken by the inspiration of the Holy Spirit in the city of Constantinople, I mean by the three hundred and eighteen that are said to have been inspired by the Holy Spirit ...

Here it is:

We believe in God the Almighty Father, Creator of things visible or invisible, and in the one Lord Jesus Christ, the only Son of God, the firstborn of all creatures, who was not made, true God of true God, of the substance of his father, by whom the worlds were established and all things were made.

Because of us men, and for our salvation, he came down from heaven, he was incarnated in the Holy Spirit and became man.

He was conceived and born of the virgin Mary.

He suffered, he was crucified in the time of Fitous, son of Kilatous (1).

He was buried and was resurrected on the third day.

He ascended into heaven, and sat down at his father's right hand: he must return a second time, to judge between the living and the dead.

We believe in the Holy Spirit, who is unique, Spirit of truth coming out of his father, Spirit who gives life; in one baptism for the remission of sins and faults; in one holy, apostolic, catholic church (we believe) that he will rise again in many bodies, and in eternal and endless life.

(1) it's fantasies and filatous (Pontius-Pilate)

Bahaeddine Al Moqtana is attached to death and resurrection on the third day of Jesus Christ.
This symbol refers to the passage from the Gospel of John which says:

"Jesus answered them (the Jews):

"Destroy this Temple, and I will restore it after" three days. "

The Jews did not want to believe that he could reestablish the Temple after three days; but he was speaking of the Temple of his body.

He reminded his disciples that he had said this, and "they believed the scriptures and his word (Gospel of John 2,19-22)".

Bahaeddine wants to give to understand that the Christians, taking these words literally, based on it their belief in the death and resurrection of the Messiah, which is an invention contrary to the design of Jesus Christ, whose disappearance must to be heard allegorically.

According to Bahaeddine, of these three days:

- the First day is the mission of the Messiah himself, at the time when the "Natiq" Jesus, son of Joseph, who was not the true Messiah, appeared.

-The Second day is the mission of the Paraclete, who is Muhammad.

For, just as Moses announced the coming of Jesus, as Jesus says in Saint John (Gospel of Saint John, 2; 19-22), Jesus also announced the advent of Muhammad.

Indeed, this is what is said in the Quran:

And [remember this:] when Jesus, son of Mary, said: "O Son of Israel! I am the Apostle of Allah [sent] to you, declaring true what, of the Torah, is prior to me and announcing an Apostle who will come after me, whose name will be Ahmad ". Now when [Jesus] came with the Evidence, [the Sons of Israel] said, "This is evident witchcraft!" (Sura 61, 6).

-The third day, is that of the mission of the Mehdi, who appeared to invite men to embrace the allegorical doctrine of "Ta'wil".

Bahaeddine adds that the Mahdi called on men to know the last day in which the Messiah was to appear.

This Messiah is Hamza, and the last day is the time of the manifestation of Intelligence, under the name and figure of Hamza.

This last day is only the complement of the first day; it is of him that the Messiah spoke saying:
"My time has not yet come" (Saint John, 7; 3-6) and it is still this day that is mentioned in the Gospel of Saint John 6: 38-40:

"I came down from heaven to do the will of him who sent me: and the will of him who sent me is that whoever will be obedient to me, I will raise them up at the last day. This is my father's will, because everyone who sees the son and believes in him has the right to eternal life, and it will be given at the last day. "

And to continue:

"O saints, do not be like those to whom Jesus said in the second section of the Gospel of John the Baptist (1):

"The light has come into the world, but men have loved darkness better than light, because their works were evil: for everyone that does evil hates the light, and does not come to the light, so that his works are not manifested; but whoever acts in a manner that is truthful, he comes to the light, so that it may be known that his works are pleasing to God. " (Gospel of Saint John 3; 19-21).

(1) We observe here that Bahaeddine confuses Saint John the Evangelist with John the Baptist!

Yet Bahaeddine was too well educated about Christianity, and knew too well the Gospels and major councils, to suppose that it was by mistake that he mistook Saint John the Evangelist for John the Baptist.

In fact his intention was to apply to a unitary missionary everything he says about Saint John the Evangelist and John the Baptist!

"Understand well, O saints, these words of the Lord which contain such marvelous traits of wisdom, and this announcement placed in the tenth section, which so positively contains the promise of his second advent.

It is when he says:

"I am the good shepherd, I know my flock, and my flock know me, as my father knows me and I know my father, and I give myself for my sheep.

I still have other sheep which are not of this fold. I must bring them, they will hear my voice, and there will be only one flock and one pastor.

That's why my father sent me, and I'm leaving my soul to take it back again. »(Gospel of Saint John 10; 14-17).

"He lets them know that the first fold is the religion of Jesus…. The other sheepfold he talks about is the religion of Muhammad. By that he promised that he would come back a second time…. He also announced his absence in the ninth section, saying: "I must do the works of him who sent me, while the day lasts; for the night will come when men can do nothing. »(Gospel of Saint John 9; 4).

[…]

As we can see in this first writing Bahaeddine Al Moqtana spares Christians in order to attract them to the Druze religion.

This will not be the case in his next two writings which are full of reproaches and invective such as for example this paragraph of his second writing entitled "Massihiyya (Christians):

"O church of impostors, where is the obedience you owe the Lord? Where is your submission to his commandments, liar men, if you believe his words, and have faith that he will come again to deliver the disciples of the truth from their sins? Did he not give you this precept in the third section of the Gospel of Matthew: "Love your enemies, bless those who curse you, do good to those who harm you, and pray for those who

…. (Gospel according to Saint Matthew 5; 44).

As we have already seen, in the "Catechism of the Druze" we find some elements concerning John the Evangelist and Christianity such as:

At the question:

Q: What is our purpose when we praise the gospel?

A: By this, we want to enhance the name of Qaim Al Hakim bi amr-allah, which is the same as Hamza; for it was he who taught the gospel.

Besides, we are obliged to approve before men of any religion whatsoever, the belief of which they profess.

Besides this, the gospel is based on divine wisdom, and its allegorical meaning is unitary religion.

Q: What should we say about the martyrs whose courage and numbers Christians praise?

A: We say that Hamza did not see fit to recognize them, that on the contrary he rejects them as apocryphal, although they have in their favor the testimony of all historians.

Q: If they tell us that the certainty of their religion is backed by evidence stronger and stronger than Hamza's word, what will we say to them? How have we known the excellence of the minister of truth, Hamza, son of Ali?

A: By the testimony that he gave to himself, when he said... "I am the first of the Lord's creatures, etc."

Q: What should we think of the gospel that is in the hands of Christians, and what is our teaching on this subject?

A: The gospel is true because it contains the word of the true Messiah, who in Muhammad's time was called Salman al Farsi, and who is Hamza, son of Ali. The false Messiah is the one who was born of Mary, for he is the son of Joseph.

Q: Where was the real Messiah while the false Messiah was with the disciples?

A: He was with him, and was among his disciples; he spoke the words of the gospel, and he instructed the Messiah, son of Joseph, prescribed to him what he should do in accordance with the laws of the Christian religion, and he listened with docility to all his words. But then having disobeyed the words of the true Messiah, he inspired the Jews to hate him, and they crucified him.

Q: What happened to him after he was crucified?

A: They put him in the tomb, but the true Messiah came, hid him from within the tomb, and hid him in the garden; then he spread the rumor among men that the Messiah had risen from the dead.

Q: Why is he doing this?

A: To establish the Christian religion, and so that men might stick to the doctrine that he (the false Messiah) had taught them.

Q: Why did he do so, so as to deceive the infidels?

A: He did so, so that the Oneness could remain hidden away from the religion of Messiah, without anyone knowing him.

Q: So who is it that rose from the grave and entered with the doors closed into the place where the disciples were?

A: It is the living and immortal Messiah, who is Hamza, the servant and slave of Our Lord Hakim.

Q: Who is it that manifested and proclaimed the gospel?

A: It is Matthew, Mark, Luke and John: it is they who are the four women of whom we have spoken.

Q: How did Christians not come to know the Unitarian religion?

A: By the operation of God, who is Al Hakim bi amr-allah.

Q: What are the Feet of the Candlestick (the candlestick on which we place the candle of the unity religion)

A: These are the 3 Warnings

Q: Who are the 3 Warnings

A: They are John, Mark and Matthew (1)

Q: For how many years have they been warning?

A: For 21 years, each of them Seven years

Q: Who are the Five Wise Virgins?

A: These are the Ministers of the Unitarian religion

Q: And what are the 5 Foolish Virgins

A: These are the Ministers of Law

(The Ministers of the Law those are those who enacted laws namely: Noah, Abraham, Moses, Issa (Jesus) and Muhammad. All are liars ".

(1) These Evangelists represent for the Druze, the NAFS, the KALIMAT and the SABIQ that is to say Ishmael, Muhammad and Abou al Kheir.

As for Luke, he represents Bahaeddine.

The True Messiah, who is Eleazar, is Hamza.

Comment:

The Druze teach a distinction between Jesus, the son of Joseph, and Christ.

Christ taught Jesus, but ultimately Jesus disobeyed Christ and was crucified.

A verse from the Qur'an speaks of "the day when the robe will be lifted up on one leg and men will be called to worship. Then the crucified is uncovered, even if previously he was hidden under a veil (68:42) ".

Christ, who was concealed as one of Jesus' disciples, stole the body of Jesus from the grave and announced that Christ had been resurrected, so that the true Druze could be concealed for a while in the religion of Jesus.

They thus join the opinion of Muslims, by denying that the Messiah was crucified, this opinion is not peculiar to Muslims.

Early Christians, Church Fathers maintained that Jesus Christ was not dead on the Cross, that it was the Holy Spirit that Jesus gave back when he spoke:

"Eloi, Eloi, lama sabachthani?" (My God, my God, why have you forsaken me?) And that we find among the four evangelists that after having pronounced these words Jesus "gave up the Spirit immediately."

It is this same Holy Spirit who came to live in the womb of the Virgin Mary and who descended on Jesus on the day of his baptism to confer upon him divine authority and power.

In the Catechism of the Druze to the question:

"What happened to him after he was crucified?

The answer is:

"They put him in the tomb, but the true Messiah came and hid him from within the tomb, and hid him in the garden; then he spread among men the rumor that the Messiah had risen from the dead. "

But according to those who maintain that Jesus Christ was not dead on the Cross, it is when it is brought down from the Cross, apparently lifeless (the blood which flowed from the wounds proved that the body was in life), but in reality unconscious, that he was transported to the garden of a rich man, Joseph of Arimatia (garden referred to by the Druze), where he was placed in a vault and that is where he received the care of the Essenes and of Mary Magdalene and the Virgin Mary.

In the Gospel of Saint John 19, 38/39 we read:

"After that, Joseph of Arimatia, who was a disciple of Jesus, but in secret out of fear of the Jews, asked Pilate for permission to remove the body of Jesus. Nicodemus also came, it is he who had previously gone to find Jesus at night. He brought a mixture of myrrh and aloe, about a hundred pounds ".

This large supply of myrrh and aloe of approximately 32 kilos and 700 grams was therefore intended for medicinal use and not to embalm the dead!

The piece of wood on which Jesus was crucified, it was other than his own who
provided and it was these others who crucified him there in the open and therefore in an exoteric way for Muslims.

By this we are given to understand that the esoteric hermeneutics unveiled by the resurrection Imam proceeds from the positive religions instituted by Envoys who were prior to the Imam of the Resurrection.

Then the Cross became an obvious theophanic sign (Ayat), for all the ranks of the initiatory hierarchy (Hôdud).

Worshiping her is an obligation incumbent on them in the same way as it is on them to venerate the Shahâdat.

Hence the comparison of the Chahâdat with the Cross.

Indeed, the Chahâdat is composed of four words:

Lâ: Imam

Illah: the Nâtiq

Illa: the Tâli

Allâh: the Sâbiq

And it is the same with the Cross which has four branches:

- The Branch which is firm in the ground: it is the counterpart of the one who is the basis of spiritual hermeneutics.

- The Branch which corresponds to it in the sense of height, in the air: it is the counterpart of the one who dispenses spiritual energy.

- The other two Branches in the middle, on the left and right sides, correspond respectively to Tâli and Natiq.

2- At the Freemasons

At the first three degrees of Freemasonry, at the Old and Accepted Scottish Rite as practiced at the Grand Lodge of France, the works are ritually and regularly opened when the Three Great Lights of the Freemasonery are placed on the altar of the Oaths.

These three Great Lights are, the Compass and the Square placed on the Volume of the Sacred Law (at the Grand Lodge of France for example it is the Bible), open to the prologue to the Gospel of John.

The masonic ritual works being of course open "to the Glory of the Great Architect of the Universe".

The Venerable asks "to reveal the three Great Lights by Opening the volume of the Sacred Law to the prologue of the Gospel of John".

Then he indicates to the audience that he will "open the works of this respectable lodge of Saint John", before finally declaring open this time "this respectable lodge of Saint John".

In some Obediences, the Lodges of the first three Degrees are called "Lodges of Saint John". We often place the open Bible on the first page of the Gospel of Saint John, sometimes referred to as the "Gospel of the Spirit", of which the first five verses - or prologue - are a true esoteric monument:

In the beginning was the Word, and the Word was with God, and the Word was God.

He was with God in the beginning. Everything, by him, has been done, and without him nothing has been done. In him was life, and the life was the light of men, and the light shines in darkness, and darkness has not received it.

The oldest Masonic rituals confirm the use of the expression "Lodge of Saint John".

Here are the questions that are still being asked of a visiting Brother when he presents himself in such a Lodge, and the answers he must give:

Revered Master: Where are you from, Brother?

Visiting Brother: From a Saint John Lodge.

The Venerable Master: What do we do in a Saint John Lodge?

Brother visitor: Wreaths are woven there for virtue; chains are forged there for vices.

Revered Master: What are you doing here?

Brother visitor: Overcome my passions, submit my will to my duties and make further progress in Masonry.

The Venerable Master: What are you bringing to the Lodge?

Visiting Brother: Kindness to all my Brothers.

And the Venerable Master, when he officially opens the Works in one of these Lodges, solemnly pronounces the following formula:

To the glory of the Grand Architect of the Universe, in the name of universal Freemasonry and under the auspices of the Grand Lodge ..., by virtue of the powers conferred on me, I declare open to the Grade of Apprentice this Respectable Loge de Saint-Jean, constituted in the East of... under the number... and the distinctive title... To me my Brothers, by the sign, the drums and the Scottish acclamation (drums: 0 - 0 - 0; acclamation: Houzé ! - Houzé! - Houzé!).

My brothers !

We are no longer in the profane world, we have left our metals at the door of the temple; let us lift up our hearts in fraternity and let our eyes turn to the Light!

f- Concept of Liberty, Equality and Fraternity

a - Among the Druze

As we have seen, what is important for the Druze is the inner conviction, the "know thyself" from which the Spirit of Truth flows.

Knowledge of the self, the "mental" stripping of everything in order to know the Absolute.

The believer follows the discipline of true-knowing, a discipline which leads him to unify and unify everything in the One.

If he entered this discipline, it was because he followed the path of Virtue, the task of achieving his goal in existence.

This conception of morality prompts the "Oneness" to appeal for equality between men.

They give equality great importance in the foundation of their morals.

As for the attitude of the "Unitarian" conception in relation to human freedom, it considers it as the result of the attitude of man, namely, so that man can achieve his goal in existence, it is necessary that he has the capacity of this realization, that he is free in his choice and in his will in what he does.

This Freedom is the basis of the Druze conception of divine justice:

If man was not free, he would not have been able to access a state of knowing which enables him to be realized in God.

Therefore, man can only conquer Paradise, which is realization in the One, through his free effort at monotheism.

Therefore the reward and the punishment are the results of the actions of the man, of what he believes, in whom he has faith and whom he follows.

Man in relation to the monotheistic conception is the summit of the world by the singularity of the evolution of his physical and mental constitution, by what distinguishes him from the point of view of capacity for evolution, understanding and discernment.

This concept of freedom, we find it throughout the history of the Druze: Opposition to the Crusaders, to the Ottomans, to the French Mandate, to Syria …

As an example, regarding the Soviet Union, Kamal Joumblatt said:

"Today many even communist parties around the world find much to fault the Moscow application of Marxist socialism.
The concept of the new historical bloc is already replacing, here and there, in practice, a system hitherto based solely on the proletariat and the principle

of the dictatorship of revolutionary power is strongly contested.

At most, it is accepted that this dictatorship can justify a strongly authoritarian government at all levels, as long as it remains respectful of essential human rights and freedoms.

These rights and freedoms are indeed for man an acquisition of inestimable importance in his historic struggle for liberation, both individual and collective.
A revolutionary power must certainly not be in a position of retrograde reaction on this plane, or it would amount to a return to the spirit of the Middle Ages.

Obviously, we are still far from it, but one day all the Communist and Socialist Parties of the world will adopt this point of view.

What is the use of bread without freedom? "

In his defense of freedom, Kamal Joumblatt was assassinated on March 16, 1977.

There is full equality between Druze men and women!

Already in Hamza's time, in Epistle 25 he broke completely with Islamic Sharia and advocated a certain emancipation of the Druze woman in matters of divorce:

"[…] I have learned that my brothers, the Sheikhs, hesitate when they must render a judgment in accordance with the prescriptions of 'assent and submission' concerning the marriage of the Oneness and the union between the brothers and the sisters: they do not know what the provisions of religion prescribe, nor what rules the conjugal union between them.

So you should know, gentlemen, that the provisions of "assent and submission" are not analogous to those of other marriage laws, for "assent and submission" are part of the orders of the Creator: whoever transgresses them opposes the command of Our Lord.

Thus, the provisions of religion require that when a Unitarian has married a Unitarian Sister, he must regard her as his equal and share with her all that he has equitably.

If circumstances force them to separate, it must be established which of the two failed in their duty to the other.

If it is the woman who shies away from the obedience she owes to her husband, although it is recognized that he is not powerless and that he treats her with justice, and that nevertheless the woman wants absolutely separate from her husband, then he will have half of everything she owns, provided, however, that people worthy of faith have attested that it was she who failed in her duty and that he was always well behaved towards her.

If, on the contrary, people worthy of faith attest that he mistreated her and that she leaves him out of necessity, she will take everything she has, without him being able to keep any thing belonging to her.
If she's the one who stood against him and refuses to go his way, he will have

half of everything she owns, even the clothes she wears on her body.

But if it is the man who decides to part with her of his own choice, without her having committed any fault towards him, then she will have half of everything he owns: clothes, furniture, money, gold, animals and anything else at his disposal, and that will come to him by law and justice.

May these gentlemen take note of this writing and retain its provisions.

Because this is how the matter must be regulated, in accordance with justice and equity [...] ”.

The Druze woman can own and dispose of her property as she pleases. Most young women under 20 go to school.

They can be initiated.

Plain and simple repudiation is not legal as we have seen among the Druze.

In addition, many Druze women have occupied prominent roles in Druze history, such as Moqtana's niece, Sarah the mother of Fakhreddin, Sitt Nassab, Sitt Hubus Arslan at the beginning of the 19th century, Sitt Na'ifa the sister by Saïd Joumblatt, Sitt Nazira the mother of Kamal Joumblatt....

Biography of Druze women who worked for the emancipation of Lebanese and Muslim women:

Nazira Joumblatt (1889-1951)

Mother of Kamal Joumblatt, Sitt Nazira took over at the age of forty, after the assassination in 1931 of her husband Fouad, the reins of the entire Druze community in Lebanon. She will work to improve her lot.

In a masculine, religious and conservative society, this woman has presided over the political majaliss (assemblies) of her country, playing a decisive role in the history of Lebanon.

She protests against the deprivation of liberty imposed on women.

Her wisdom, her perspicacity, her high moral authority made her respected by all communities.

Nazira Zeinedinne (1908-1976)

She is one of the most important Arab writers of her time and who is committed against what she considers to be degrading practices of her culture.

In addition to her criticism of the full veil worn by Muslim women during this time, she is also known for her outspokenness about the exclusion of women.

Her writings are seen by feminists as necessary answers to the topic of veiling in the Middle East at the time.

Women are then not allowed to leave their homes without having their faces covered, and there is no question of religious choice on their part.

For feminists, the full veil is seen as a source of oppression and exclusion serving the logic of male domination

She spends much of her life writing and defending the identity and equality of women in the Arab world.

His work therefore had a great impact on the Muslim community.

She is one of the first women to use the Qur'an to overturn notions the Muslim clergy defend as arising from these same texts.

She thus questions the validity of misogynistic interpretations made of sacred texts.

She then calls on each believer to make their own judgment about what is moral and what is not.

She inspires many Muslim women to take control of their own bodies, their education and most importantly, their lives.

b - Among the Freemasons

Liberty, Equality, Fraternity

This is the last sentence uttered by the Venerable Master for the opening and closing of the work of the Old and Accepted Scottish Rite (REAA).

The words: Liberty, Equality, Fraternity form the motto by which the Freemason is inspired in his behavior in the Temple and in his action in the secular world.

This motto adorns the Orient of the Lodge.

It is also the fundamental motto of the Republic and the primary concept of the Declaration of the Rights of Man and of the Citizen.

This concept is the very foundation of any democracy in the world.

Freedom is never definitively acquired.

It must be the object of constant vigilance on the part of the Freemason to continue to enlighten the world.

Freedom preexists in relation to society.

The individual, alone like the hermit, is in essence free.

The notion of freedom as we know it takes on its full meaning and grandeur in the social context.
One of the maxims of the Republic says in this regard that freedom is limited

only to that of others.

Freedom is fully expressed in Freemasonry:

Indeed, the Freemason is free to continue or not the process he has taken.

In Freemasonry, the jewel of the Senior Warden is a perpendicular therefore a vertical axis, just like the representation of the number "One".

Responsible for the education of entered-apprenticed, it seems normal that he is associated with freedom, the first step on the path to light.

The entered-apprenticed ritual specifies in fact that "the free man is the one who, after having died to the prejudices of the vulgar, has seen himself reborn to the new life conferred by initiation".

Equality:

The concept of equality is necessarily dependent on comparison: one can only be equal in relation to something or to someone.

As much as freedom can exist in nature, equality is a purely intellectual and therefore human construction.

Animals are not concerned with this consideration: on the contrary, it is often the hierarchy that guarantees the survival of the species (see natural selection). Man, for his part, has taken as a fundamental principle in the declarations of human rights "equality under the LAW".

In nature, the only equality that exists is that of all living things in the face of the certainty of death.

Living things are not naturally equal. They are complementary or interdependent.

Most of the time, they form a coherent whole.

The food chain is a perfect illustration of this.

Like her, the Freemasons' own Chain of Union continues to exist despite the disappearance of some of its links. These are replaced by others.

Note that the mathematical symbol of equality consists of two horizontal and parallel lines.

This horizontality is also present in Freemasonry in the jewelry of the First Supervisor, which consists of a level.

The ritual also says that the level symbolizes for the mason the leveling of inequalities, a task to which he must strive.

The fraternity sums up all the duties of Freemasons towards others.

It means: dedication, abnegation, tolerance, benevolence, indulgence.
Fraternity is a very strong bond between individuals who are different by race,

religion etc. and which includes reciprocal recognition.

Good is not only good for me but for everyone.

Chapter VI

Famous Druze Freemasons

Freemasonry has never been condemned by a Druze religious Sheikh.

According to Druze social and religious values, Freemasonry is not a betrayal of oneness (Tawheed) since it is part of the worldly elements.

It therefore does not interfere with the religious sphere reserved only for initiates.

The double belonging of a secular Druze (Jahil) to Freemasonry cannot therefore pose an identity crisis.

For him, who is far from the demand for religious initiation, Freemasonry can constitute a substitute for properly religious initiation.

This requires total availability and can only be done under very specific conditions.

In addition, for "Jahil", there is a concordance of principles between the two Universes: the Masonic Universe and the Unitary World (Muwahidin) of the Druze.

Freemasonry can remind the layman Druze of elements of his religion: he can identify with it.
As we have seen, the Druze religion and Freemasonry find elements in common, notably, let us recall it in the theory of emanations, that of the uniqueness of being and the belief in the immortality of the 'soul etc ...

The intellectual heritage of the two Orders is the same: the Druze regard

Pythagoras, Plato and Aristotle as Druze prophets just as they are regarded by the Freemasons as Masons without aprons.

And in the 17th degree rituals of the Ancient and Accepted Scottish Rite (REAA) which has the title: "Knight of the East and the West", we learn from the Freemason that its origin dates back to the year 1180, period to which the Western Crusaders united with the Eastern Masons (the Druze), true disciples of John of Patmos (Saint John) under the leadership of Gaumont, Patriarch of Jerusalem.

Some historians go even further, claiming that the title of the 22nd degree of the Scottish Rite, "Prince of Lebanon" refers to the followers of this symbolic religion.
In the ritual of 22 ° the Very Wise addresses the Speaker:

"Brother Orator, please read the Oath of the Knights Royal Arch"

The Speaker:

On this Volume of the Sacred Law, deposit of the faith of the followers of Virtue, I... .. I renew expressly and without any restrictions all the commitments that I have already contracted.

I swear to give up everything to follow the Princes of Lebanon, my Brothers, and to work my entire life on the rebuilding of the Temple, using the precious tool entrusted to me. So helps me the Great Architect of the Universe.

The Druze is a unifying factor among Freemasons in the Middle East.

Some Druze personalities
who belonged to Freemasonry

ABOU CHAKRA Daoud (1884-1940)

Born in Ammatour in the Chouf in Lebanon, he entered Freemasonry in 1914.

He was known to have refused to have his religion mentioned in the 1922 census and insisted that he be mentioned "without religion".

ABOU CHAKRA Nassib (1884-1940)

A freemason like his father Daoud, he was a journalist before joining the Police to become the first Chief of the Judicial Police in Lebanon.

He represented his country for several years in the offices of Interpol International in charge of the office of narcotics.

ABOU CHAKRA Kamil

Born in Ammatour in the Chouf in Lebanon, he was in the years 1936, Venerable Master of the lodge "Al Marj" in the East of Beirut under the jurisdiction of the Grand Lodge of New York.

ARSLAN Adel (Emir) - 1889-1954

Thinker and politician, the Emir Adel Arslan belonged to a family of Freemasons: his father, his older brother, and especially the Emir Mohammed Amine Arslan, founder and president of the First Lodge of Beirut.

He pushed the lodges to serve the Arab cause and was elected Grand Master, in order, he says, to save Freemasonry from Jewish influence.

So he wanted to implement this policy and during a meeting of the Syrian and Lebanese lodges, in his opening speech he said:

If I accepted to be Grand Master it is to contribute to the Arab cause and if Freemasonry in this country helps this cause then it is blessed, otherwise it no longer has reason to exist.

He had been promoted to the 33rd degree as Emir Abdel Kader, Hajj Hussein Beyhoum of the "Palestine 415" lodge, Emir Mohammed Arslan, Emir Melhem Arslan (Caïmacam du Chouf), doctor Youssef Jalkh, Nassif Jezzini , Mikhaël Nehmé, Nicolas Medawar...

ARSLAN Amin (Emir) - 1868 -1943

Born in 1868 in Choueifat in Lebanon from a family of notables of the Druze faith, the Emir (Prince) Amin Arslan studied with the Jesuit Fathers in Beirut before becoming a Freemason.

He was initiated at the age of 21, on August 24, 1889 at the lodge "Le Liban" in the Orient of Beirut under the jurisdiction of the Grand Orient of France.

Appointed Consul General of the Ottoman Empire in Bordeaux then in Paris, he was one of the first to denounce the genocide of the Armenians.

ARSLAN Chakib (Emir) – 1869 - 1946

Nicknamed "Prince of Eloquence" for his mastery of the Arabic language, he was an influential historian, politician, poet and writer.

Famous Arab-Islamic nationalist is at the origin of the newspaper "The Arab Nation" which influenced many Arab nationalist leaders, in particular the Maghreb separatists.

In 1932 he became an important member of Action Marocaine and took as secretary a Freemason Thami El Ouazzani.

He would have been initiated in the 1930s in the Grand Orient of Spain.

ARSLAN Melhem (Emir)

He belonged at the end of the 19th century to the Palestine Lodge in the East of Beirut and was elevated to the 33rd degree of the Old and Accepted Scottish Rite.

ARSLAN Mohammed (Emir)-1838-1869

Caïmacam (Prefect) of the Druze in Mount Lebanon, State Councilor in Constantinople, he founded the Syrian Scientific Society, a foundation which brought together men of all religions and all political allegiances.

He was also the Founder and President of the first Masonic lodge in Lebanon, the "Palestine" lodge in the East of Beirut and elevated to the 33rd degree of the Old and Accepted Scottish Rite.

ARSLAN Magid (Emir)- 1908-1983

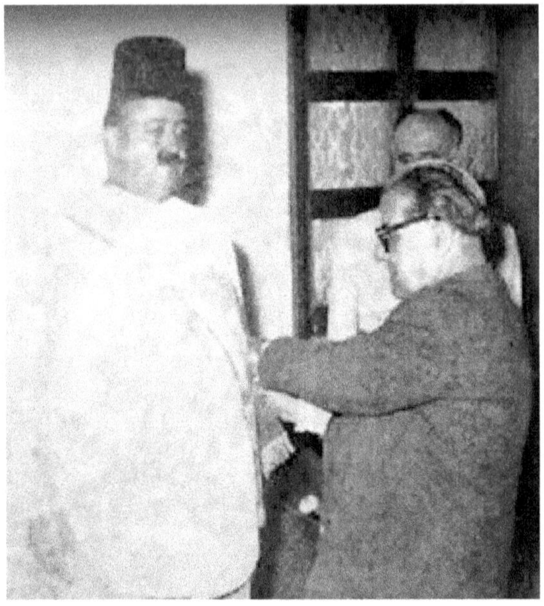

Emir Magid Arslan receiving the 33rd insignia from Grand Master Hanna Abi Rached

He was one of the founders of the independence of Lebanon and was several times minister and holder of several decorations.

In 1949, during a ceremony at his palace in Khaldé near Beirut and in front of a delegation of "world freemasonry", he received from the hands of the Grand Master of the Ideal Grand Lodge of the Lebanese Republic, Grand Master Hanna Abi Rached, the badge of the 33rd degree as well as the title of Honorary Grand Master

A Lodge in Lebanon from the beginning of the 20th century bears the name of "AL ARSLAN N ° 86".

HAMADE Amin

Born in Aïtat in the Chouf (Lebanon), he was 33 ° of the REAA and in 1947 became the First Vice-President of the Lebanese Grand Lodge for Lebanon and the Arab Countries.

JOUMBLATT Mahmoud

Former member of the Lebanese Administrative Council, he opposed with six members of this Council the creation of a Greater Lebanon.
It belonged in the early 1900s to the "Sannine" Lodge in the East of Dhour el Choueir (Lebanon) under the jurisdiction of the Grand Lodge of Scotland.

TAKIEDDINE Mahmoud

Civil inspector, born in 1867 in Baakline (Lebanon), he was initiated at the age of 25, on March 4, 1892, at the Lodge "Le Liban" in the East of Beirut, under the jurisdiction of the Grand Orient of France and belonged in the early 1900s to the Lodge "Sannine" in the East of Dhour el Choueir (Lebanon) under the jurisdiction of the Grand Lodge of Scotland.

Bibliography elements

ABOU ZAKI Nadine, "Introduction to the Epistles of Wisdom" Paris, Harmattan, 2006

ABDELHAMID Mohamed, "Sabi'at Houran Wa Al Tawhid Al Durzi", Damas, Dar el Tali "at, Al Jadida, 2000

ARACTINGI Jean-Marc, "History of Freemasonry in the Middle East (Lebanon, Syria, Palestine, Turkey, Egypt, Iran ..) ", 706 pages - 2019- Amazon CreateSpace Independent Publishing Platform

ARACTINGI Jean-Marc, "Esoteric and spiritual Islam in 7 lessons", (2017 - Amazon Kindle Direct Publishing)

ARACTINGI Jean-Marc, "The Ecumenical Rite (Judeo-Christian-Muslim) in Freemasonry
Volume I "(2017 - Amazon Kindle Direct Publishing)

ARACTINGI Jean-Marc and LOCHON Christian, "Islam and Freemasonry-Esoteric Traditions", Éd. Edilivre-Paris, 2014

AZIZ Philippe, "The secret sects of Islam", Paris, Laffont, 1983

AZZI Joseph, "Between Reason and the Prophet", Paris, Bertoin, 1992

BARAKAT Leila, "Under the Vines of the Druze Country", Paris, Harmattan, 1993

BERNARD Raymond, "Encounters with a secret order: the Druzes" Ed. Rosicruciennes, 1976

BLAVASTKY Hélène: The Letters of HP Blavatsky, Vol. 1, Letter n ° 110, 1861-79.

BOIVIN Michel, "Les Ismaéliens", Belgium, Editions Brepols, 1998

BOURON Captain, "The Druzes, History of Lebanon and the Hauranese Mountain", Paris, 1930

BURCKHARDT Titus, "Introduction to the esoteric doctrines of Islam", Paris, Derain, 1955

CALLEBAUT Paul-Jacques, "The mysterious Druzes of Mount Lebanon" Belgium, La Renaissance du Livre, 2000

CALLEBAUT Paul-Jacques and Nicole, "Rites and Mysteries in the Middle East", Paris, Laffont, 1980

CARBILLET Capitaine, "Au Djebel Druze, things seen and lived", Paris, Argo, 1929

CHASSEAUD G. W., "The Druzes of Lebanon, Their Manners, Customs and History", London, 1855

CHURCHILL Charles Colonel, "The Druzes and The Maronites", London,

1862

From SMET D. "The Sacred Epistles of the Druze" (Vol.1 & 2), Paris, Peeters, 2007

From SMET Daniel, "La Philosophie Ismaélienne", Éd. Deer 2012

DUPONT Marie, "Les Druzes", Belgium, Brepols, 1994

GUYS Henri, "La nation Druze", Paris, 1863

HATEM Jad, "God as a Man in Druzism", Librairie de l'Orient-Paris, 2006

IBN ARABI, "Les Révélations Mecquoises: Futûhat" 4 volumes Paris, Sindbad, 1989

JOUMBLATT Kamal, "For Lebanon", Ed.Sock1978

JOUMBLATT Kamal, Interview with the Lebanese newspaper L'Orient-le Jour in 1970

LOCHON Christian, "Interview with Lebanese Druze personalities" in "Secrets of initiation into Islam and masonic rituals" by Jean-Marc ARACTINGI and Christian

LOCHON, Ed. L'Harmattan-Paris-2008

MAKAREM Sami Nassib, "The Druze Faith", Delmar, New York, 1974

MAKAREM Sami Nassib, "Al-'Irfan Fi Maslak al-Tawhid (Ad-Durziyya)", Druze Heritage Foundation, London, 2006

MARQUET Yves, "The Philosophy of Ikhwan al Safa", H.E.H.A. Paris and ARCHE Milan, 1999

MASSIGNON Louis, "Essay on the origins of the technical lexicon of Muslim mysticism", Amazon
PERILLIER Louis, "Les Druzes", Paris, Publisud, 1986

RIVOAL Isabelle, "The Masters of the Secret", Paris, EHESS, 2000

SACY de Sylvestre, "Exposé de la Religion des Druzes", Paris, 1840

SPRINGETT Bernard, "Secret Sects of Syria and the Lebanon", USA, Forgotten Books, 2011

TAKIEDINNE Zeinedinne Cheikh, "The Book of Points and Circles", Beirut, Dar el Nachr, 1999

YASSIN Anwar, "Catechism of the Druzes", Paris, Esoterikos, 1985